RADNOR HUNT

THE FOX'S KITCHEN

CHERISHED RECIPES *from* PHILADELPHIA'S HISTORIC RADNOR HUNT

BY RADNOR HUNT
MEMBERS & FRIENDS

A RADNOR HUNT COOKBOOK

PHOTOGRAPHS BY BRIAN DONNELLY

Mrs. Moran's Brushwood Stables

The Fox's Kitchen is dedicated to ELIZABETH "BETTY" MORAN, a longtime member of Radnor Hunt and a great devotee to the importance of open space—we shall forever treasure her contributions!

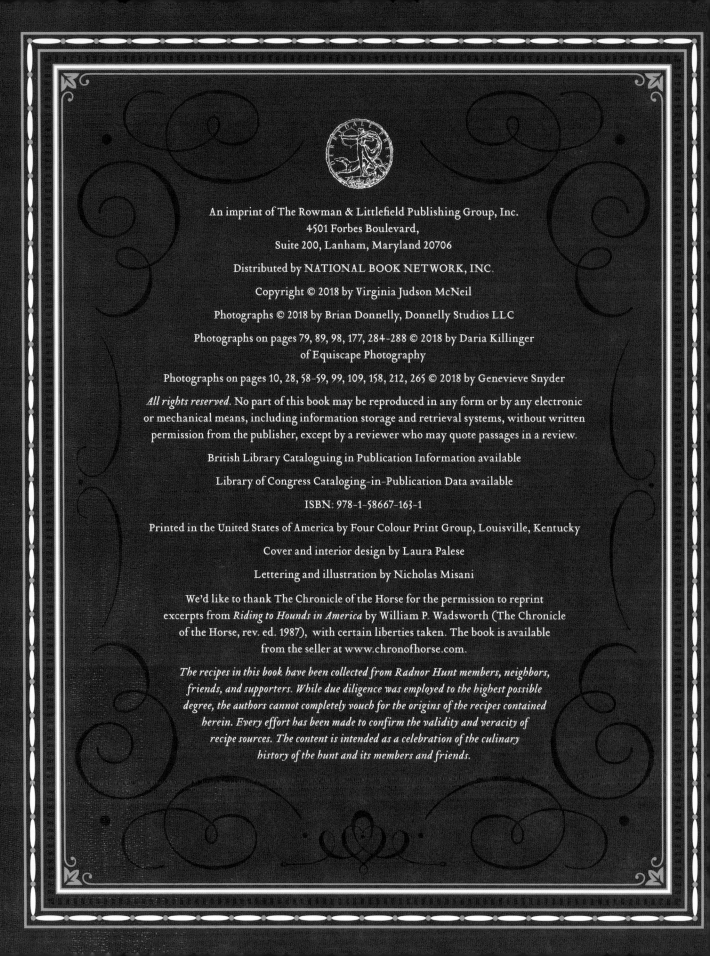

An imprint of The Rowman & Littlefield Publishing Group, Inc.
4501 Forbes Boulevard,
Suite 200, Lanham, Maryland 20706

Distributed by NATIONAL BOOK NETWORK, INC.

British Library Cataloguing in Publication Information available

Library of Congress Cataloging-in-Publication Data available

ISBN: 978-1-58667-163-1

Printed in the United States of America by Four Colour Print Group, Louisville, Kentucky

Cover and interior design by Laura Palese

Lettering and illustration by Nicholas Misani

We'd like to thank The Chronicle of the Horse for the permission to reprint
excerpts from *Riding to Hounds in America* by William P. Wadsworth (The Chronicle
of the Horse, rev. ed. 1987), with certain liberties taken. The book is available
from the seller at www.chronofhorse.com.

*The recipes in this book have been collected from Radnor Hunt members, neighbors,
friends, and supporters. While due diligence was employed to the highest possible
degree, the authors cannot completely vouch for the origins of the recipes contained
herein. Every effort has been made to confirm the validity and veracity of
recipe sources. The content is intended as a celebration of the culinary
history of the hunt and its members and friends.*

THE HOUNDS FOUNDATION

exists to perpetuate an understanding of the country way of life,
promote land conservation, maintain and preserve the
history and traditions of hunting with hounds, and educate the public
on proper hound breeding and care. In this context, the
foundation is pleased to work with the Brandywine Conservancy,
the Brandywine Red Clay Alliance, the French & Pickering
Creeks Conservation Trust, Natural Lands, the Willistown Conservation
Trust, the Chester County Historical Society, Greener Partners,
and the Cheshire Land Preservation Fund.

ALL NET PROCEEDS FROM *THE FOX'S KITCHEN* WILL GO TO SUPPORT THE HOUNDS FOUNDATION.

WE WOULD LIKE TO ACKNOWLEDGE

OUR

Sponsors

MASTERS CIRCLE

Franny and Franny Abbott

Mr. and Mrs. Collin F. McNeil

FIRST FLIGHT

Brandywine Conservancy

Brandywine Red Clay Alliance

Maripeg Bruder

Bryn Mawr Trust

Richard S. Caputo, Esquire of
Fox Rothschild LLP

Cheshire Land Preservation Fund

Chester County Historical Society

French & Pickering Creeks
Conservation Trust

Greener Partners

Mr. and Mrs. J. Wesley Hardin

The Kraut Family

Mr. and Mrs. Britton H. Murdoch

Natural Lands

Dr. and Mrs. Donald J. Rosato

George and Helen Sipala

Yvonne and Brock Vinton

Janice and Cortright (Cortie)
Wetherill, Jr.

Willistown Conservation Trust

SECOND FLIGHT

Jerome R. Keough

Mike DeHaven, Rainer & Company

THIRD FLIGHT

The Costello Family
Christina and Steve Graham
Anne Hamilton
Patty and Peter Irish

Mary MacGregor Mather and
Charles E. Mather III
Dorothy Mather Ix and
Raymond E. Ix, Jr.

Mr. and Mrs. Charles E. Mather IV
Edward and Nicole Riegl
Mr. and Mrs. Gary Warzecha

HILL TOPPERS

A.J. Blosenski, Inc., Trash
& Recycling Service
Arader Tree Service, Inc.
Barnyard Products, LLC
Maggie and Andy Cappelli
The Caulfield Family
Eileen M. Corl
Kathy Craven
Lisa and Sanford Davne
John and Biddy Day
Esther and Paul Gansky
Gardner's Landscape & Nursery

Ray and Patsy Jones
Peggy Mason
Stephanie and John McGowan
Mr. and Mrs. Robert Patterson
Eleanor Reeve Peterson
Pickering Valley Feed & Farm Store
Amanda and Conrad Radcliffe
Ron's Original Bar & Grille
Lynn and Anthony C. Salvo
Melissa Scheppele
Christa and Calvin W. Schmidt

Mr. and Mrs. Douglas D. Schroer
Trudy and James Simpson and
Family
Stephen Sordoni
Mr. and Mrs. Randal Steinhoff
Synergy Sports & Corrective
Massage, LLC
Michael G. Tillson III
James and Bonnie Van Alen
Sharon Vinton
Walter J. Cook Jeweler
Peter and Eliza Zimmerman

CAR FOLLOWERS

Archer & Buchanan Architecture
Joy Atwell
Mrs. Sandra K. Baldino
Thaddeus Bartkowski
Angi Bevers
Broad Run Farm
Jennifer N. Cahill
Mr. and Mrs. Edward Cook III
Eric and Helen Corkhill
Bryn Devine
The Dougherty Family
Ann and Brad Dyer
Mr. and Mrs. John A. Eichman IV
Amos Fenstermacher
Brook Gardner and Jodi Spragins
Jean Good
Marlou and John Gregory

Jeffory A. Griffin-Grossi
JoAnn Wallis Harley
Kirk and Sandy Harman
Barbara Hill
Steve and Sharon Holt
L. Stockton and Eleanor Morris
Illoway
Anna Kreuzberger
Leslie Lindsley
Mrs. Thompson A. Maher
Ralph W. Marsh
Peggy Matje
Ron and Barbara Mattson
Wade and Wendy McDevitt
Mr. and Mrs. A. David McGinnis III
Deborah S. McKechnie, ex-MFH

Mr. and Mrs. Robert S.
McMenamin
Harper Meek and Kris Bartosiak
Mr. and Mrs. Carl Meister
Amanda Barnes Muckle
Blaire Baron Pew and Derek Pew
Marcia Pontius
Nancy R. Schwab
Holly and John Stoviak
Linda Sturgeon
Lance, Debra, and Adare Taylor
Deborah S. Terzian
Gary M. Tocci
Avis K. Tsuya
Peter and Lisa Waitneight
Col. and Mrs. R.B. Wiltshire
Ethel B. Wister

CONTENTS

PREFACE 12 • RADNOR HUNT: A BRIEF HISTORY 14

A NOTE ON HOW TO USE THIS BOOK 21

THE MENUS

ONE
Opening Meet Celebration
24

TWO
Fox's Feast
46

THREE
Tailgate Party
60

FOUR
Fox & Hound Fireside Meal
82

FIVE
Full of the Moon Roundtable
96

SIX
Dogs' Dinner
114

SEVEN
Supper at the Pub
128

EIGHT
Full Cry Dinner
152

NINE
Bitches' Brunch
166

TEN
Masters' Menu
184

ELEVEN
Spring Fling
198

TWELVE
Tallyho, Let's Eat!
214

THIRTEEN
Radnor Fete
228

FOURTEEN
The Huntsman's Gathering
246

FIFTEEN
Cubbing Summer Supper
260

GLOSSARY OF HUNTING TERMS & PHRASES 276

ACKNOWLEDGMENTS 280 • INDEX 284

PREFACE

IT'S NO SECRET THAT FOXHUNTERS LOVE A GOOD PARTY, A GOOD DRINK, AND ESPECIALLY GOOD FOOD.

Whether it's contained in a pewter flask or in a crystal port glass; whether it's served on a paper plate or on Wedgwood porcelain; whether it's a post-hunting tailgate, hunt breakfast, or dinner for twelve, Radnor Hunt has always epitomized the best of eating, drinking, and making merry!

To celebrate this long devotion to food and drink, members and friends of the hunt have published this work. Recipes from the kitchens around hunt country have been collected, and, in some cases pried away, from the chefs, cooks, and mixologists who have long been devotedly preparing their fare. All entries have been tested by a panel of expert gluttons. *The Fox's Kitchen* is a reflection of the intersection between a beloved sport and the country living and entertaining Radnor Hunt fully embraces.

Michael G. Tillson III, MFH • *Collin F. McNeil, MFH*
Esther B. Gansky, MFH • *J. Wesley Hardin, MFH*

RADNOR HUNT

RADNOR HUNT
A Brief History

RADNOR HUNT *is the oldest continuously active foxhunting club in the United States, recognized by the Masters of Foxhounds Association of America.*

Every September since the hunt's founding day, December 16, 1883, there has been a Radnor hunting season—this despite two world wars and several lesser ones, financial depressions, disagreements over hound breeding, landowner issues, Prohibition, and the insidious creep of urban sprawl. The hunt's roots lie in the country life that sprang up outside Philadelphia along the storied Main Line, where the wealthy established themselves. Foxhunting was seen as a proper diversion for gentlemen and ladies, and many Philadelphia area hunts were formed.

Leading citizens, including successful industrialists, top attorneys, architects, and other professionals, assumed important roles in the club through the decades. Notable in the years of suburban growth, which unceasingly brought about the demise of many other hunting operations, Radnor persevered. A combination of forward thinking, flexibility, tenacity, and devotion ensured the hunt's continuity.

Foxhunters leaving Radnor Hunt on Opening Day,
November 15, 1932, which was the first season in
Malvern, Pennsylvania, with the new stables pictured

*Radnor ladies hunting
sidesaddle, 1919*

Thanksgiving Day, 1981

Throughout the end of the nineteenth century and into the early
years of the twentieth, the exploits of Radnor Hunt were regularly
recounted in Philadelphia newspapers. The Thanksgiving Day hunt and
associated Hunter Trials and Races attracted large crowds of onlookers
who would drive their carriages—and later their motorcars—to the
club to enjoy a day of sport. Even World War I, to which many hunt
members answered the call to duty, didn't imperil hunting and racing.
However, the postwar encroachment of suburbia and attendant growth
of the membership led the hunt's leadership to consider new country,
farther afield. Radnor had been hunting regularly "up-country" in
parts of Tredyffrin, Easttown, and Willistown Townships. Led by
members Benjamin Pew, Horace Hare, and Edward Beale, and joined
by the newly affiliated Master Roy Jackson (shown on pages 84–85), the
hunt purchased the old Gallagher Farm on Boot Road (now Providence
Road) in White Horse, Pennsylvania. Hunt member Arthur Meigs, of the
renowned Philadelphia architectural firm of Mellor, Meigs & Howe, was

Radnor's newly constructed
kennels, 1932

Fixture card denoting
Hunt Meets, 1939

Longtime Huntsman
Will Leverton, 1928

commissioned to oversee renovations to the farmhouse and the design and construction of new stables and kennels. The Hunt moved to its present location in 1931.

Since that time, foxhunting (actually fox *chasing*, since the fox is revered and preserved, to provide for another day's sport) has been conducted three days a week from September through March on farms in the Willistown countryside surrounding the club. Members also enjoy hunting in the beautiful rolling hills along the Brandywine Creek of the Old Brandywine hunt territory. Devotees of the sport, on any given hunt day, will number from twenty to nearly seventy-five on horseback, with quite a few following on foot and by car.

The centuries-old sport of foxhunting is replete with flashes of scarlet coats, the cry of hounds, the shine of an expertly groomed horse, and the camaraderie engendered by mutual enjoyment of the "old habit"—an arm around a shoulder, a glass of fine port, stories of exploits embellished. Out of this life have come these long-loved recipes. Out of this life has come this book.

THIS PAGE, CLOCKWISE FROM TOP: *The first Radnor Hunt clubhouse, 1894; Radnor's original Huntsman, John Mather, 1884; Edward Beale, an original member of Radnor, rode to hounds for 65 years; MFH Horace Hare, 1924; Master and Field managing a gate, 1919*

THIS PAGE, CLOCKWISE FROM TOP: *Charles E. Mather,
MFH Radnor Hunt, 1895 (center), with hounds and staff
on the lawn at Avonwood, his country home in Haverford,
Pennsylvania; Master and Huntsman William Evans with
his hounds, 1960; hounds at the original kennels, 1912*

Table designed by Valley Forge Flowers

A NOTE ON
How to Use This Book

I n *The Fox's Kitchen*, we share more than one hundred of our most cherished recipes, organized into fifteen menus that exemplify our verve for gatherings, ranging from small, intimate fireside dinners to grand Opening Meet celebrations. Tried and trusted, these dishes are ones we make again and again. The meals we've assembled—some lavish, some casual—are how we like to entertain: graciously and practically. You won't find any complicated techniques or daylong preparations in this book. We like to be relaxed and at ease when our guests arrive, and we want you to feel the same.

Many of the menus include a generous number of dishes. These meals are intended to be shared—often by many. Some menus serve four to six; others have higher yields and are meant for larger parties of, say, ten or twelve. Feel free to mix and match recipes from the different menus, but be sure to check the yields and reduce or increase quantities within the recipes accordingly. The dishes we present are some of our favorites, collected from a wide cross section of Radnor Hunt members, neighbors, friends, and supporters, and the menus are designed with the hunting season in mind, beginning with our Opening Meet, which takes place in November, continuing through to winter, then spring, and ending with Cubbing, which brings us to late summer and early fall.

FOXHUNTING ETIQUETTE

Given its age and origins, the sport of foxhunting has accumulated a bounty of required "uniforms," best practices, and mandated or understood behaviors. You will find Foxhunting Etiquette tips throughout, which are intended to illuminate these mostly practical, but somewhat curious traditions. And toward the back of the book you'll find a Glossary of Hunting Terms & Phrases. Please use it to reference any hunting jargon unfamiliar to you. Whether this book is your first introduction to our club or you're a long-time member, we hope our grand passion for food and hunting is evident!

CHARLIE'S TIPS

When you spy a fox, all brilliant reddish orange, with resplendent brush (tail) and angular white and black mask (face) tipped by a sharp black nose, he doesn't know who you are, but you should definitely know who he is. Charlie is his name. In fact, be it a dog, vixen, or cub, it is called Charlie—or "Charles James Fox" in more formal terms. Why? During the reign of King George III, who presided over those pesky colonials causing such troubles for the Crown, there was a prominent member of the House of Commons by the name of Charles James Fox, who was one of the most influential characters of Parliament in the late eighteenth and early nineteenth centuries. He was a staunch opponent of the king and a great advocate of the American Revolution, even dressing in the colors of George Washington's army. Just as wild foxes caused trouble for farmers, ravaging henhouses and sheep pens, Charles James Fox was considered to be a rascal and rabble-rouser by the king and his Tory supporters. Following Fox's death in 1806, the golden age of foxhunting literature commenced. Novels and hunt accounts of the time began to regularly refer to the hunted quarry as "Charlie." Reviled by some, championed by others, Charlie it is, and alway will be! In the spirit of Charlie, various recipes throughout the book include a "Charlie's Tip," which may be a hint, suggestion, or other useful information pertaining to the dish at hand. Wild, wise, and wonderful, who better than Charlie to preside over his own kitchen?

Charles James Fox

OPENING MEET CELEBRATION

Blackberry-Rosemary Rum Cocktail 26

Sweet & Spicy Mixed Nuts 29

Easy Fig Spread 30

Tomato, Cannellini & Rosemary Soup 33

Arugula & Macadamia Salad with Green Goddess Dressing 34

Grilled Loin Lamb Chops with Mint Pesto 38

Golden Potato Gratin 41

Candied Carrot Cake 42

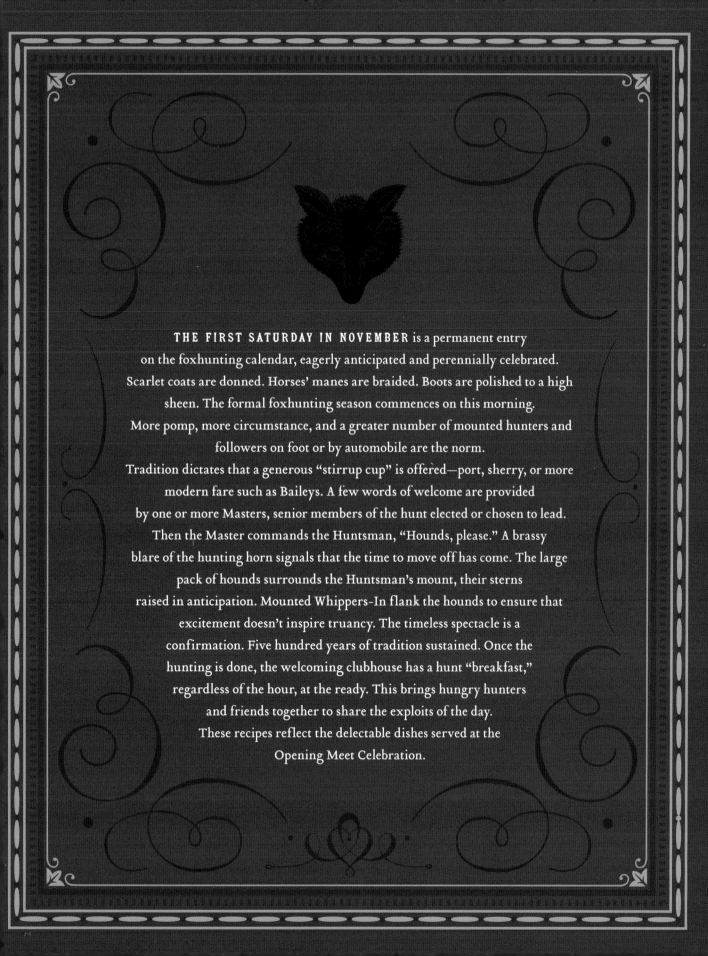

THE FIRST SATURDAY IN NOVEMBER is a permanent entry
on the foxhunting calendar, eagerly anticipated and perennially celebrated.
Scarlet coats are donned. Horses' manes are braided. Boots are polished to a high
sheen. The formal foxhunting season commences on this morning.
More pomp, more circumstance, and a greater number of mounted hunters and
followers on foot or by automobile are the norm.
Tradition dictates that a generous "stirrup cup" is offered—port, sherry, or more
modern fare such as Baileys. A few words of welcome are provided
by one or more Masters, senior members of the hunt elected or chosen to lead.
Then the Master commands the Huntsman, "Hounds, please." A brassy
blare of the hunting horn signals that the time to move off has come. The large
pack of hounds surrounds the Huntsman's mount, their sterns
raised in anticipation. Mounted Whippers-In flank the hounds to ensure that
excitement doesn't inspire truancy. The timeless spectacle is a
confirmation. Five hundred years of tradition sustained. Once the
hunting is done, the welcoming clubhouse has a hunt "breakfast,"
regardless of the hour, at the ready. This brings hungry hunters
and friends together to share the exploits of the day.
These recipes reflect the delectable dishes served at the
Opening Meet Celebration.

Blackberry-Rosemary
RUM COCKTAIL

※ *Makes 1 drink* ※

Handful of ice

2 ounces amber rum

1 ounce Blackberry-Rosemary
Syrup (recipe follows)

4 ounces seltzer water

Fresh blackberries, for garnish

Sprig of fresh rosemary, for garnish

Fill a highball glass with ice. Add the rum and Blackberry-Rosemary Syrup. Pour in the seltzer and stir. Garnish with a few fresh blackberries and the rosemary. Serve immediately.

BLACKBERRY-ROSEMARY SYRUP

Makes 1½ cups (enough for 12 cocktails)

1 cup fresh or frozen blackberries

1 tablespoon coarsely chopped
fresh rosemary

1 cup turbinado sugar

In a small saucepan, combine the blackberries (no need to thaw them if they're frozen), rosemary, sugar, and 1 cup water. Using the back of a wooden spoon, gently press the blackberries against the side of the pan to crush them. Bring the mixture to a boil over medium-high heat and cook, stirring occasionally, until the sugar has dissolved, about 3 minutes. Remove the pan from the heat and allow the mixture to steep for 2 hours. Pour the syrup through a fine-mesh strainer into an airtight container and discard the solids. Cover and store in the refrigerator for up to 2 weeks or in the freezer for up to 3 months.

Blackberry-Rosemary
Rum Cocktail with
Sweet & Spicy Mixed
Nuts (page 29)

Sweet & Spicy
MIXED NUTS

Makes 6 cups

Nonstick cooking spray

1 cup sugar

2 teaspoons sea salt

1 teaspoon ground cumin

1 teaspoon ground cinnamon

1 teaspoon freshly ground black pepper

¼ to ½ teaspoon cayenne pepper

6 cups unsalted mixed nuts (pecans, cashews, etc.; about 20 ounces)

2 large egg whites, beaten until frothy

Preheat the oven to 325°F. Spray two rimmed baking sheets with cooking spray.

In a large bowl, whisk together the sugar, salt, cumin, cinnamon, black pepper, and cayenne. Add the nuts and egg whites and toss to coat.

Divide the nuts between the prepared baking sheets and spread them into a single layer. Bake, stirring occasionally, until the nuts just start to turn golden and are almost dry, 20 to 25 minutes. Remove from the oven and let the nuts cool completely before serving.

Store in an airtight container for up to 2 weeks or in the freezer for up to 3 months.

CHARLIE'S TIP

The nuts may seem a bit moist when they come out of the oven, but as they cool, they'll continue to dry. Because these nuts freeze well, we love to double or triple the recipe so we always have some on hand. If you do this, however, don't crowd the pans— instead, bake the nuts in several batches to ensure they toast evenly.

Easy
FIG SPREAD

≫ Makes 2 cups ≪

1¼ cups dry red wine, such as
    Merlot

1½ cups dried Black Mission figs
    (about 8 ounces), stemmed and
    halved

1 dried bay leaf

¼ teaspoon aniseed

In a small saucepan, combine the wine, figs, bay leaf, and aniseed. Bring the mixture to a gentle boil over medium heat, reduce the heat to low, and simmer for 15 minutes, or until the figs are rehydrated and soft. Remove the pan from the heat and allow the mixture to cool.

Discard the bay leaf, transfer the mixture to a food processor, and puree until smooth. Store in an airtight container in the refrigerator for up to 2 months.

CHARLIE'S TIP

*A great kitchen staple, fig spread is the perfect
accompaniment to cheese and crackers, makes a delectable crostini spread,
and is also delicious stirred into a bowl of yogurt.*

Tomato, Cannellini & Rosemary
SOUP

⚞ Serves 4 to 6 ⚟

2 tablespoons extra-virgin olive oil

1 yellow onion, chopped

2 carrots, peeled and chopped
(about 1 cup)

2 garlic cloves, chopped

1 (15-ounce) can cannellini beans,
drained and rinsed

1 (28-ounce) can crushed tomatoes

3 cups chicken broth

1 dried bay leaf

2 teaspoons minced fresh rosemary

½ teaspoon red pepper flakes

½ teaspoon sea salt, plus more to taste

½ teaspoon freshly ground black
pepper, plus more to taste

⅔ cup crème fraîche, for serving

Zest of 1 lemon, for serving

In a large Dutch oven, heat the olive oil over medium-high heat until it starts to shimmer. Add the onion, carrots, and garlic and cook until the vegetables are just becoming soft, about 4 minutes. Add the beans, tomatoes, chicken broth, bay leaf, rosemary, red pepper flakes, salt, and black pepper. Increase the heat to high and bring the soup to a boil, then reduce the heat to low, cover, and simmer for 30 minutes. Remove from the heat and let cool slightly.

Discard the bay leaf. Working in batches, carefully transfer the soup to a blender and puree until smooth (be careful when blending hot liquids). Taste and season with more salt and black pepper as desired. If needed, reheat the soup over low heat.

To serve, ladle the soup into individual serving bowls and garnish each with crème fraîche and a sprinkle of lemon zest.

CHARLIE'S TIP

This soup freezes particularly well. We like to use resealable freezer bags, because they lie flat and save freezer space. Be sure to let soups cool completely before freezing.

Arugula & Macadamia
SALAD
WITH GREEN GODDESS DRESSING

⟨ Serves 4 to 6 ⟩

1 red bell pepper, seeded and cut into thin strips

8 ounces baby portobello mushrooms, cut into quarters

5 ounces baby arugula

⅓ cup macadamia nuts, toasted (see Charlie's Tip)

¼ cup Green Goddess Dressing, plus more to taste (recipe follows)

Sea salt and freshly ground black pepper

In a large bowl, combine the bell pepper, mushrooms, arugula, and macadamia nuts. Drizzle with the Green Goddess Dressing and toss to combine. Add more dressing, if desired, and toss again. Season with salt and pepper and serve immediately.

CHARLIE'S TIP

Toasting nuts heightens their flavor and also makes them crunchier.
To toast nuts on the stovetop, place the nuts in a dry skillet and heat over medium heat, stirring or shaking the pan continuously, for 3 to 4 minutes. Because of their high fat content, nuts tend to burn easily, so take the pan off the heat as soon as you see the nuts turning lightly golden—or when you smell a fragrant, toasted aroma. Use your sight and nose to judge doneness. Immediately transfer the toasted nuts to a bowl or plate, as they will continue to cook in the heated pan even if it's off the heat, and let cool.

RECIPE CONTINUES

"Huntsman and Hounds" statue by Radnor Hunt member Kathie Friedenberg

GREEN GODDESS DRESSING

Makes 1½ cups

½ cup buttermilk

¼ cup mayonnaise

¼ cup sour cream

4 scallions, white and green parts, coarsely chopped

½ cup chopped fresh chives

⅓ cup packed fresh basil leaves

¼ cup packed flat-leaf parsley leaves

2 tablespoons chopped fresh dill

1 tablespoon fresh thyme leaves

2 garlic cloves

2 tablespoons fresh lemon juice, plus more to taste

½ teaspoon sea salt, plus more to taste

¼ teaspoon freshly ground black pepper

Place all the ingredients in a blender or food processor and puree until smooth. Taste and add more lemon juice and/or salt as needed. Store in an airtight container in the refrigerator for up to 2 weeks.

FOXHUNTING ETIQUETTE

- *Arrive at the hunt with a well-groomed horse and clean tack. You are representing our hunt. If you bring a guest, introduce him or her to the Field Master and Master.*

- *The field follows and obeys instructions from the Field Master. It is important for the field to remain in a group so the riders are not spread out to potentially turn the fox or be in the Huntsman's way. Do not follow the Whippers-In, as they are not part of the field. (If, however, you do get separated from the rest of the field, it is better to follow a Whipper-In to rejoin the field than to strike off on your own and risk spoiling the sport for all.)*

Grilled Loin
LAMB CHOPS
WITH MINT PESTO

Serves 4

8 (1-inch-thick) lamb loin chops (about 2 pounds)

2 tablespoons extra-virgin olive oil

Sea salt and freshly ground black pepper

1½ cups Mint Pesto (recipe follows), for serving

Preheat a stovetop grill pan over medium heat or heat an outdoor grill to medium.

Rub the lamb chops with the olive oil and season them generously with salt and pepper. Place the lamb chops in the hot pan or on the grill and cook to the desired doneness, about 4 minutes per side for medium-rare. Transfer to a cutting board and let rest for 5 to 8 minutes, then top each chop with a spoonful of the Mint Pesto and serve.

MINT PESTO

Makes 1½ cups

2 cups loosely packed fresh mint leaves

⅓ cup slivered almonds

⅓ cup coarsely grated Parmesan cheese (about 1½ ounces)

1 tablespoon fresh lemon juice

1 garlic clove

½ cup plus 2 tablespoons extra-virgin olive oil

Sea salt and freshly ground black pepper

In a food processor, combine the mint, almonds, cheese, lemon juice, and garlic. Pulse several times, then, with the motor running, slowly add the olive oil through the feed tube. Process until smooth. Taste and season with salt and pepper. Store in the refrigerator for up to 2 days.

Golden
POTATO GRATIN

⸻ Serves 10 ⸻

3 tablespoons unsalted butter, plus more for the pan

3 large red onions, thinly sliced

6 Yukon Gold potatoes, peeled and thinly sliced (about 6 cups)

1½ teaspoons sea salt

Freshly ground black pepper

12 ounces Emmental cheese, coarsely grated (about 4½ cups)

2 cups heavy cream

In a large skillet, melt the butter over medium heat until it just begins to foam. Add the onions and cook, stirring occasionally, until they become translucent, 3 to 4 minutes. Reduce the heat to medium-low and cook, stirring often, until the onions become golden brown, 30 to 40 minutes more. If the onions become too brown on the edges, reduce the heat a bit more. If the moisture from the onions has evaporated and it seems the onions may burn, add a few tablespoons of water.

Meanwhile, preheat the oven to 375°F. Butter a 9 x 13-inch glass baking dish.

Layer one-third of the potatoes, evenly and slightly overlapping, in the bottom of the prepared baking dish. Season with ½ teaspoon salt and pepper to taste, then spread one-third of the onions evenly over the potatoes and sprinkle with one-third of the grated cheese. Repeat to make a second layer of the potatoes, salt and pepper, onions, and cheese. Layer on the remaining potatoes and season with the remaining salt and pepper to taste. Using an offset spatula, press down on the potatoes, then pour the cream evenly over the top until it just reaches the top of the layer. Top with the remaining onions and sprinkle evenly with the remaining cheese. Bake for 45 minutes, or until the potatoes are fork-tender and the top is bubbling and golden brown. Remove from the oven and serve.

Candied
CARROT CAKE

⁓ Makes one 9-inch cake ⁓

FOR THE CAKE

¾ cup vegetable oil, plus more for the pans

2 cups all-purpose flour, plus more for the pans

2 teaspoons ground cinnamon

2 teaspoons baking soda

½ teaspoon sea salt

2 cups granulated sugar

¾ cup buttermilk

3 large eggs, beaten

2 teaspoons pure vanilla extract

2 cups grated carrots

1 cup pecans or walnuts, chopped

1 (8-ounce) can crushed pineapple, drained

1 cup sweetened flaked coconut

½ cup golden raisins

FOR THE BUTTERMILK GLAZE

1 cup granulated sugar

½ cup buttermilk

½ cup (1 stick) unsalted butter

1 tablespoon light corn syrup

½ teaspoon baking soda

1 teaspoon pure vanilla extract

FOR THE CREAM CHEESE FROSTING

1 (8-ounce) package cream cheese, at room temperature

½ cup (1 stick) unsalted butter, at room temperature

3½ cups confectioners' sugar

1 teaspoon pure vanilla extract

1 cup finely chopped pecans, toasted (see Charlie's Tip, page 34), for garnish (optional)

Make the cake: Preheat the oven to 350°F. Grease three 9-inch round cake pans with oil and dust them with flour, tapping out any excess.

In a medium bowl, whisk together the flour, cinnamon, baking soda, and salt. Set aside. In a large bowl, stir together the granulated sugar, buttermilk, oil, eggs, and vanilla and beat well. Add the dry ingredients and mix until thoroughly combined. Using a rubber spatula, fold in the carrots, nuts, pineapple, coconut, and raisins. Divide the batter among the prepared pans.

RECIPE CONTINUES

*Radnor Member J. Stanley Reeve
smartly turned out for Opening Meet, 1922*

CANDIED CARROT CAKE
CONTINUED

Bake the cakes for 35 to 40 minutes, until a wooden toothpick or skewer inserted into the center of each cake comes out clean.

While the cakes are baking, make the buttermilk glaze: In a saucepan, combine the granulated sugar, buttermilk, butter, corn syrup, and baking soda. Bring to a boil over medium heat and cook, stirring frequently, for 4 minutes. Remove the mixture from the heat and stir in the vanilla.

Set a wire rack over a rimmed baking sheet. Transfer the cakes to the rack and let cool slightly, about 10 minutes, then invert them onto the rack. Immediately spoon the buttermilk glaze over them and let the glazed cakes cool completely.

Meanwhile, make the cream cheese frosting: In a large bowl using a handheld mixer, beat the cream cheese and butter on medium speed. Reduce the speed and gradually add the confectioners' sugar. Beat until light and fluffy. Add the vanilla and mix to combine.

Trim the tops of the cakes to level them, if desired, then set one cake layer upside down on a serving plate. Frost the top of the cake, then set a second cake layer on top and frost that as well. Set the final cake layer upside down on top and frost the top and sides of the cake. If desired, gently pat the pecans onto the frosted sides of the cake before slicing and serving. Store in the refrigerator, covered, for up to 5 days. Bring to room temperature before serving.

FOX'S FEAST

Polo Punch 48

Artichoke & Caper Dip 51

Spinach Salad with Paprika Dressing 52

Truffle Pasta 55

Chocolate Chip Pecan Oatmeal Cookies 56

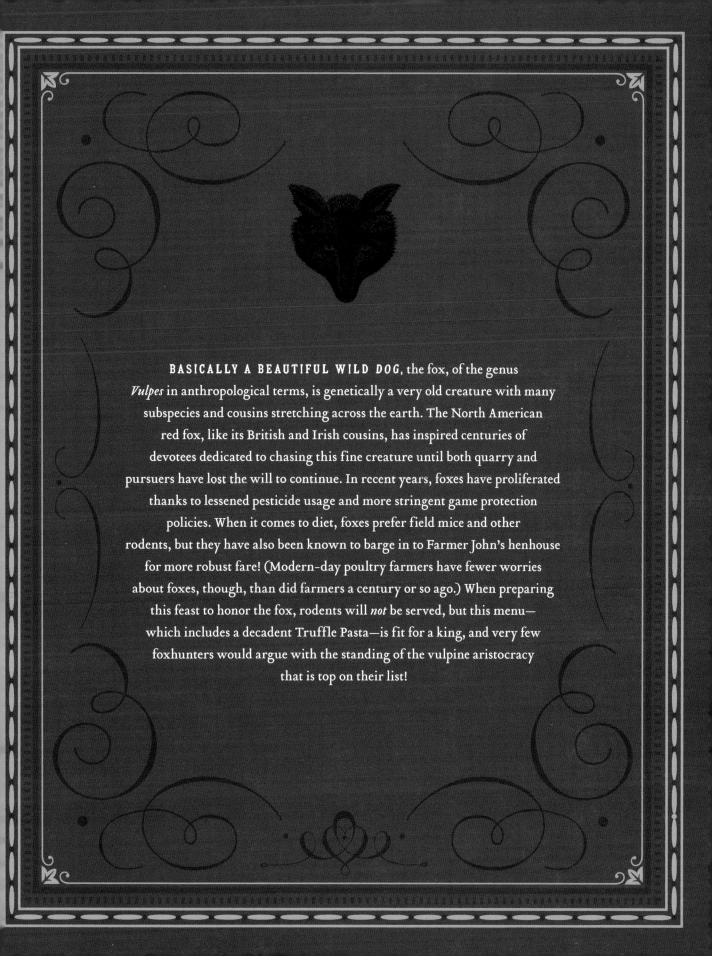

BASICALLY A BEAUTIFUL WILD DOG, the fox, of the genus *Vulpes* in anthropological terms, is genetically a very old creature with many subspecies and cousins stretching across the earth. The North American red fox, like its British and Irish cousins, has inspired centuries of devotees dedicated to chasing this fine creature until both quarry and pursuers have lost the will to continue. In recent years, foxes have proliferated thanks to lessened pesticide usage and more stringent game protection policies. When it comes to diet, foxes prefer field mice and other rodents, but they have also been known to barge in to Farmer John's henhouse for more robust fare! (Modern-day poultry farmers have fewer worries about foxes, though, than did farmers a century or so ago.) When preparing this feast to honor the fox, rodents will *not* be served, but this menu— which includes a decadent Truffle Pasta—is fit for a king, and very few foxhunters would argue with the standing of the vulpine aristocracy that is top on their list!

Polo PUNCH

※ *Serves 8* ※

**FOR THE LEMONADE
(SEE CHARLIE'S TIP)**

½ cup honey

2¼ cups steaming-hot (almost boiling) water

1½ cups fresh lemon juice (from about 9 lemons)

FOR THE PUNCH

12 ounces Pimm's No. 1

8 ounces vodka

2 lemons, cut into ¼-inch-wide rounds

About 4 cups ice

Make the lemonade: In a heatproof 1-quart measuring cup or bowl, combine the honey and hot water. Stir until the honey has dissolved. Stir in the lemon juice. Cover and refrigerate for a few hours until cold, or until you're ready to serve.

Make the punch: In a large pitcher, combine the lemonade, Pimm's, vodka, and halve the lemon rounds, cutting a slit in each one. Fill eight highball glasses or ½-pint mason jars with ice and divide the punch among the glasses. Garnish each glass with a lemon slice. Serve immediately.

CHARLIE'S TIP

Before squeezing the lemons, heat them in the microwave for about 10 seconds per lemon and then, with your hand, roll each one back and forth on the countertop. The result of this process is a greater juice yield from each lemon.

Don't want to make your own lemonade? You can substitute a quart of lightly sweetened premade lemonade.

THE RADNOR HUNT

OWNER
1958 ALFRED H. SMITH
1959 ALFRED H. SMITH
1960 MRS WALTER SCHAUM
1961 JOHN SCHAUM
1962 MARY G. STEPHENSON
1963 GEORGE A. WEYMOUTH

1964 GEORGE A. WEYMOUTH
1965 D. L. FERGUSON
1966 MRS GEORGE W. RUTTON
1967 REDMOND C. STEWOLD
1968 MRS. MARGARET H. WOS
1969 JOHN W. WARNER
1970 STUART G. JANNEY
1971 FRANK A. BONSAL
1972 SHILOH FARMS
1973 H. TURNEY McKNIGHT

PILOT–JAMES F. SIMPLER
ER–MRS. HENRY STERN
ER–MRS. HENRY STERN
MAN AUGUSTIN STABLES
STATION GREGORY S. BENTLEY
NG INTEREST AUGUSTIN STABLES
LLIVAN Mrs. THOMAS H. VOSS
LLIVAN Mrs. THOMAS H. VOSS
WHISTLE PHOENIX STABLE
E'S DEWAN Mrs. F. EUGENE DIXON, Jr.
ART PARCEL LANDSLIDE FARM
AHEAD KINROSS FARM
IRVIN S. NAYLOR
UATTHEEVENT ARTHUR W. ARUNDEL
E BIANCO (IRE) ARTHUR W. ARUNDEL

Artichoke & Caper Dip wth
Polo Punch (page 48)

ARTICHOKE & CAPER
Dip

⚜ *Makes 2 cups* ⚜

1 garlic clove

2 (14-ounce) cans artichoke hearts, drained

3 ounces capers (about ½ cup), drained

Zest and juice of 1 lemon

8 to 10 fresh basil leaves

2 tablespoons extra-virgin olive oil, plus more as needed

Sea salt and freshly ground black pepper

Baguette slices, toast, or bagel crackers, for serving

In a food processor, pulse the garlic until finely chopped, scraping down the sides of the bowl with a spatula as needed. Add the artichoke hearts, capers, lemon zest, lemon juice, and basil. Pulse several more times until just combined. With the motor running, slowly add the olive oil through the feed tube until the mixture comes together but is still chunky. Do not overprocess into a paste.

Transfer the dip to a serving bowl. Taste and season with salt and pepper. Serve with baguette slices, toast, or bagel crackers. Store in an airtight container in the refrigerator for up to 1 week.

CHARLIE'S TIP

This dip makes a delicious sandwich spread and is also great tossed with warm pasta.

SPINACH SALAD

WITH PAPRIKA DRESSING

Serves 6

4 large eggs

1 pound baby spinach

10 slices bacon, cooked and cut into bite-size pieces

1 medium red onion, thinly sliced

½ cup Paprika Dressing (recipe follows)

Sea salt and freshly ground black pepper

Place the eggs in the bottom of a pot and cover with water. Bring the water to a boil over high heat, then remove the pot from the heat and cover. Allow the eggs to sit in the water for 13 minutes. Meanwhile, fill a bowl with ice and water. After the eggs have rested in the water, drain them and place them in the ice water to cool for 5 minutes. Drain again and set aside.

Put the spinach, bacon, and red onion in a large bowl and toss with the Paprika Dressing. Peel and chop the hard-boiled eggs and place them on top of the salad. Season with salt and pepper. Serve.

PAPRIKA DRESSING

Makes about 1 cup

1 egg yolk

2 tablespoons sugar

1 tablespoon Worcestershire sauce

1½ teaspoons paprika

¼ teaspoon dry mustard

½ teaspoon sea salt

¼ teaspoon freshly ground black pepper

¾ cup neutral oil, such as canola

¼ cup red wine vinegar

In a food processor, combine the egg yolk, sugar, Worcestershire, paprika, mustard, salt, and pepper and pulse just to combine. With the motor running, slowly add the oil through the feed tube and process until smooth. With the motor running, add the vinegar and process until emulsified. Store in the refrigerator for up to 1 day.

Truffle PASTA

1 tablespoon sea salt, plus more
    to taste

2 tablespoons extra-virgin olive oil

2 tablespoons unsalted butter

3 ounces black truffle pâté

5 anchovy fillets, patted dry and
    finely chopped, or 1 tablespoon
    anchovy paste

5 garlic cloves, finely chopped

¼ teaspoon red pepper flakes

¼ teaspoon freshly ground black
    pepper, plus more to taste

1 pound campanelle or cavatappi
    pasta

⅔ cup finely grated Parmesan or
    Pecorino Romano cheese (a scant
    1½ ounces), plus more for serving

3 tablespoons chopped fresh parsley

Fill a large pot with water and add the salt. Bring to a boil over high heat.

Meanwhile, in a large skillet, heat the olive oil and butter over medium-high heat until the butter foams. Add 2 ounces (about ¼ cup) of the truffle pâté, the anchovies, garlic, red pepper flakes, and black pepper and cook, stirring, until fragrant, about 1 minute. Remove from the heat and set aside.

Add the pasta to the boiling water and cook according to the package directions until just al dente. Using a fine-mesh strainer or frying spider, transfer the pasta directly to the skillet with the pâté mixture, reserving the pasta water in the pot.

Return the skillet to the stovetop, add ¼ cup of the pasta cooking water, and heat over medium heat, using tongs to gently toss the pasta until the sauce thickens slightly and coats the pasta. If needed, add more pasta water, 1 teaspoon at a time, until you reach the desired consistency.

Remove the pan from the heat, sprinkle with the cheese and parsley, and toss.

Taste and season with salt and pepper.

Divide the pasta among six serving bowls. Garnish with the remaining 1 ounce truffle pâté, spooning a small amount on top of each serving. Serve immediately, passing extra grated cheese at the table.

Chocolate Chip Pecan
OATMEAL COOKIES

Makes 6 to 7 dozen cookies

1 cup (2 sticks) unsalted butter, at room temperature, plus more for the pans

2 cups all-purpose flour

1 teaspoon coarse sea salt

1 teaspoon baking soda

1 teaspoon baking powder

1 cup packed brown sugar

1 cup granulated sugar

2 teaspoons pure vanilla extract

2 tablespoons milk

2 large eggs

2½ cups old-fashioned rolled oats

12 ounces semisweet chocolate chips (about 2 cups)

1½ cups chopped pecans

Preheat the oven to 350°F. Grease two rimmed baking sheets with butter.

In a medium bowl, whisk together the flour, salt, baking soda, and baking powder. (The key to this cookie is the coarse sea salt. Don't even think about skipping it!) Set aside.

In the bowl of a stand mixer fitted with the paddle attachment, cream the butter and sugars on medium-high speed for 3 minutes, or until light and fluffy. Add the vanilla, milk, and eggs and beat on medium until incorporated, stopping and scraping down the sides of the bowl with a rubber spatula as needed. Add the dry ingredients and beat on low until just combined. Stir in the oats, chocolate chips, and pecans by hand.

Using a tablespoon measure, form the dough into rounded balls and place them 1½ inches apart on the prepared baking sheets.

Bake for 10 to 12 minutes. Remove the cookies from the oven before they look fully cooked, as they will continue to cook on the warm baking sheet. Let cool on the pans for 3 to 5 minutes, then transfer to wire racks to cool completely before serving. Store in an airtight container for up to 5 days.

The sun rising over Radnor Hunt and its historic racecourse

MENU THREE

TAILGATE PARTY

Planter's Punch 62

Retro Molded Egg Salad Appetizer 65

Texas Caviar Dip 68

Roasted Corn Salad 70

Chicken Cashew Chili 73

Fresh Layered Salad 74

Caramel & Sea Salt Brownies 77

English Flapjacks 81

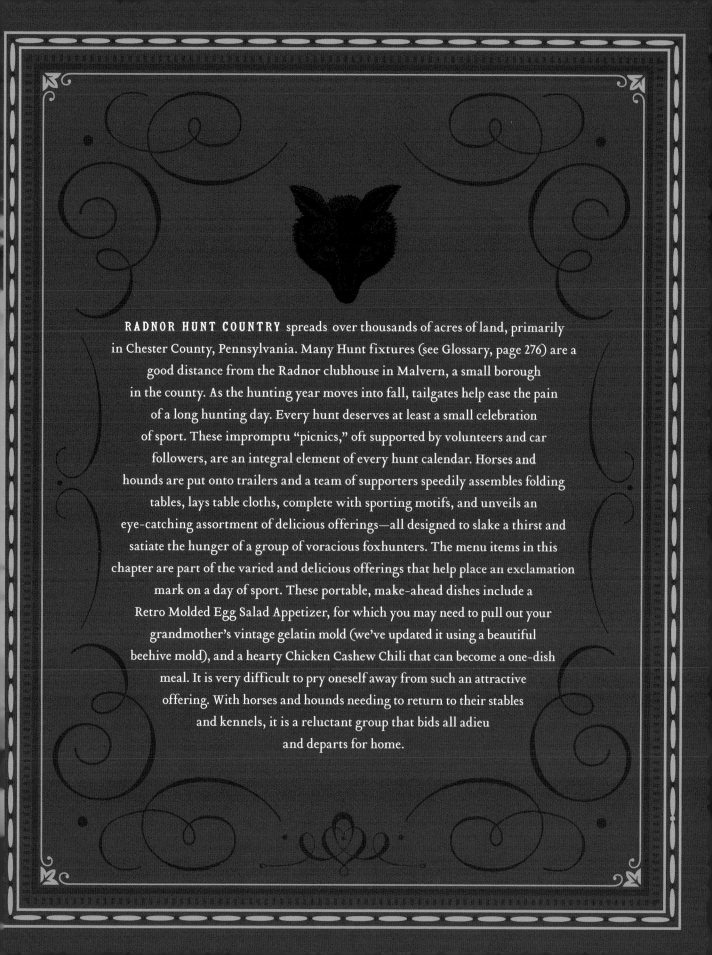

RADNOR HUNT COUNTRY spreads over thousands of acres of land, primarily in Chester County, Pennsylvania. Many Hunt fixtures (see Glossary, page 276) are a good distance from the Radnor clubhouse in Malvern, a small borough in the county. As the hunting year moves into fall, tailgates help ease the pain of a long hunting day. Every hunt deserves at least a small celebration of sport. These impromptu "picnics," oft supported by volunteers and car followers, are an integral element of every hunt calendar. Horses and hounds are put onto trailers and a team of supporters speedily assembles folding tables, lays table cloths, complete with sporting motifs, and unveils an eye-catching assortment of delicious offerings—all designed to slake a thirst and satiate the hunger of a group of voracious foxhunters. The menu items in this chapter are part of the varied and delicious offerings that help place an exclamation mark on a day of sport. These portable, make-ahead dishes include a Retro Molded Egg Salad Appetizer, for which you may need to pull out your grandmother's vintage gelatin mold (we've updated it using a beautiful beehive mold), and a hearty Chicken Cashew Chili that can become a one-dish meal. It is very difficult to pry oneself away from such an attractive offering. With horses and hounds needing to return to their stables and kennels, it is a reluctant group that bids all adieu and departs for home.

Planter's
PUNCH

꿏 Makes 1 drink 꿏

2 ounces Mount Gay Eclipse or other amber rum

2 ounces fresh pineapple juice

2 ounces fresh orange juice

Juice of ½ lime (about 1 tablespoon)

2 teaspoons Homemade Grenadine (recipe follows)

Handful of ice

Freshly grated nutmeg, for garnish

Slice of lime, for garnish

Maraschino cherry, for garnish

Combine the rum, pineapple juice, orange juice, lime juice, and Homemade Grenadine in a shaker and shake for 10 seconds. Fill a highball glass with ice and pour the cocktail over it. Garnish with fresh nutmeg, the slice of lime, and a maraschino cherry. Serve.

HOMEMADE GRENADINE

Makes ¾ cup

¼ cup sugar

1 cup unsweetened pomegranate juice

½ lemon (optional)

In a small pot, combine the sugar and pomegranate juice and heat over medium-high heat, stirring, until the sugar dissolves. Bring the mixture to a rapid boil and cook for 5 minutes or until slightly thickened. Don't boil it for too long, or it will crystallize. Remove the syrup from the heat and let cool completely. Taste and, if desired, add a few drops of lemon juice to bring out the tartness. Store in an airtight container in the refrigerator for up to 1 month.

EGG SALAD

APPETIZER

❧ Serves 24 to 30 ❧

12 large eggs

3 (1-ounce) packets unflavored
    powdered gelatin

2 cups mayonnaise

½ cup finely chopped celery

½ cup finely chopped scallions
    (white parts only)

½ cup chopped sweet gherkin
    pickles

¼ cup chopped pimentos

¼ cup finely chopped red bell
    pepper

1 teaspoon sea salt

½ teaspoon white ground pepper

Nonstick cooking spray

1 (8-ounce) package cream cheese

½ cup sour cream

Whole and sliced almonds, for
    garnish

Party pumpernickel or crackers, for
    serving

Place the eggs in a single layer in the bottom of a large pot and add enough water to cover them by 2 inches. Bring the water to a boil over high heat, then remove the pot from the heat and cover. Allow the eggs to sit in the water for 12 minutes. Meanwhile, fill a large bowl with ice and water and set it nearby. After the eggs have rested in the water, drain them and place them in the ice water to cool for 5 minutes. Drain them again, then gently crack, peel, and chop them. Set aside.

Pour 1 cup water into a medium saucepan and place over low heat. Sprinkle with the gelatin. When the gelatin has dissolved, remove the pan from the heat. Whisk in the mayonnaise, celery, scallions, pickles, pimento, bell pepper, salt, and white pepper. Fold in the chopped eggs.

Spray an 8-cup mold (see Charlie's Tip, page 66) with cooking spray and fill it with the egg mixture. Cover and refrigerate overnight.

RECIPE CONTINUES

RETRO MOLDED EGG SALAD APPETIZER
CONTINUED

The next day, in a small bowl, stir together the cream cheese and sour cream until smooth. Transfer the mixture to a pastry bag fitted with a medium star tip. Remove the salad from the refrigerator.

To unmold the salad, carefully run a knife around the top edge to loosen it. Place a serving platter on top of the mold and gently invert the mold and platter together. Starting at the base of the molded salad, pipe continuous rings of the cream cheese mixture around the salad until it's entirely covered. Decorate with "bees" made out of whole almonds with sliced almonds for wings. Serve with party pumpernickel or crackers.

CHARLIE'S TIP

We love to use a beehive cake pan as a mold for this salad.
You can also use an 8-cup stainless steel bowl to achieve a similar beehive effect.
Retro Jell-O molds and rings make fun presentations, too.

- **FOXHUNTING ATTIRE** *is grounded in tradition, but that tradition is firmly based upon practicality. It has developed over the years to keep riders comfortable in the weather and field conditions that one is likely to encounter in the fall, winter, and early spring. Further, for many who participate in or watch the hunt, including landowners and their families, the spectacle of a nicely turned-out field is pleasurable and indicates our respect for both the traditions of the sport and the landscape to which we have been granted access. The details of acceptable attire vary somewhat from region to region and hunt to hunt. Some hunts are quite particular about certain nuances of turnout (for example, finding square or colored saddle pads unacceptable), so if hunting elsewhere, a polite inquiry as to any special considerations may be in order. The guidelines given here apply to adult hunt attire for the Radnor Hunt.*

- *Formal hunt attire is worn beginning with the Opening Meet in November. Once the formal season commences, hard hats and high boots should be black. (Note that patent boot tops for ladies or brown boot tops for gentlemen should only be worn if one has been awarded one's hunt colors.) Riding coats should be black or navy (for women), and worn with beige, tan, canary, or rust-colored breeches. Riding shirts should be white or canary with a white stock tie. The tie should be affixed with a simple stock tiepin running horizontally. (A pin running vertically is reserved for staff.) It is recommended that you affix the ends of your stock tie to your shirt with two small safety pins hidden inside your coat—flapping stock tie ends are both unsightly and a safety hazard. A vest (traditionally canary or tattersall plaid) may be worn once the weather gets colder, but should not be viewed as required if the weather is warm.*

TEXAS CAVIAR
Dip

⚶ Serves 10 ⚶

1 small red bell pepper (see Charlie's Tip)

½ cup extra-virgin olive oil, plus more for brushing

¼ cup apple cider vinegar

¼ cup sugar

1 (15-ounce) can black beans, drained and rinsed

1 (15-ounce) can black-eyed peas, drained and rinsed

1 cup fresh corn kernels (see Charlie's Tip)

¼ cup finely chopped red onion

1 jalapeño, seeded and finely chopped

2 celery stalks, chopped

2 tablespoons chopped fresh cilantro

Tortilla chips, for serving

Preheat the broiler. Lay the bell pepper on a baking sheet and brush it thoroughly with olive oil. Place the pan under the broiler; after 5 minutes or so, areas of the skin should start to char. When this happens, use tongs to flip the pepper and broil until the skin blisters on the second side as well. After about 8 minutes, transfer the pepper to a heatproof bowl, cover the bowl with a plate, and let sit for 10 minutes or so. Peel the pepper (the skin will slip right off), then cut it into quarters. Discard the stems and seeds, then finely chop the flesh and set aside.

In a small saucepan, combine the olive oil, vinegar, and sugar. Heat over medium heat, stirring occasionally, until the sugar has dissolved, then remove from the heat.

In a large bowl, combine the beans, black-eyed peas, corn, onion, jalapeño, celery, cilantro, and roasted red pepper. Sprinkle with the oil-vinegar mixture and toss to combine. Cover and refrigerate overnight or for at least 4 hours, stirring a few times.

Remove the dip from the refrigerator about 30 minutes before serving and allow it to come to room temperature. Drain some or all of the liquid. Serve with tortilla chips. Store in an airtight container in the refrigerator for up to 3 days.

CHARLIE'S TIP

You could use ½ cup drained and chopped jarred roasted red peppers here instead of roasting one (just skip this step).

If the corn is perfectly fresh, you can eat it cut straight off the cob. If it needs a little refresher, though, cook it in salted boiling water for 1 to 3 minutes and immediately submerge it in ice water to stop the cooking, then cut the kernels from the cob once it has cooled. You will get about 1 cup corn kernels from one large or two medium cobs.

Roasted
CORN SALAD

1 teaspoon sea salt, plus more for the cooking water

12 ears white or bicolor fresh corn, husked

1 red onion, cut into small dice

½ cup fresh basil, coarsely chopped, plus more for garnish

¾ cup (1½ sticks) unsalted butter, melted

2 tablespoons Champagne vinegar

½ teaspoon sugar

Freshly ground black pepper

Bring a large pot of salted water to a boil over high heat. Fill a large bowl with ice and water and set it nearby. Add the corn to the boiling water and cook for 1 to 3 minutes, then immediately submerge them in the ice water to stop the cooking. When cool enough to handle, cut the kernels from the cobs.

Put the corn kernels in a large bowl and add the onion, basil, melted butter, vinegar, salt, and sugar. Toss to combine. Taste and season with pepper. Serve at room temperature. Garnish with basil just before serving.

CHARLIE'S TIP

This salad can be made a day in advance and stored in the refrigerator (without the basil garnish). Bring to room temperature before serving.

Chicken Cashew
CHILI

2 cups chicken broth

4 dried ancho chiles, stemmed, seeded, and crumbled

1½ cups unsalted cashews

¼ cup extra-virgin olive oil

2 large onions, chopped

6 garlic cloves, chopped

2 tablespoons ground cumin

2 teaspoons chili powder

2 teaspoons sea salt

8 boneless, skinless chicken breasts (about 3 pounds)

6 tablespoons chopped fresh cilantro

2 (14.5-ounce) cans diced tomatoes

2 ounces good-quality bittersweet chocolate

2 (15-ounce) cans kidney beans, drained and rinsed

In a small saucepan, bring the chicken broth to a boil over high heat. Add the chiles, then remove from the heat and let soak for 10 minutes. Transfer the chiles and broth to a blender and add ½ cup of the cashews. Puree until smooth; set aside.

In a large heavy-bottomed Dutch oven, heat the olive oil over medium heat. Add the onions and garlic, and cook, stirring occasionally, until softened, about 7 minutes. Sprinkle the onion-garlic mixture with the cumin, chili powder, and salt, stir to combine, and cook for 1 minute more. Add the chicken and stir to coat.

Pour in the reserved chile puree, 3 tablespoons cilantro, and the tomatoes with their juices. Bring to a simmer over medium-low heat, cover, and cook, stirring occasionally to avoid sticking, for 45 minutes, or until the chicken is cooked through.

Remove the pot from the heat and, using tongs, transfer the chicken to a bowl. Set aside to cool. Using two forks or your hands, shred the meat. Return the shredded chicken to the pot and stir in the remaining 1 cup cashews, chocolate, and beans.

Cook the chili over medium heat until the chocolate has melted and the stew is heated through. Serve immediately, or let cool completely, transfer to an airtight container, and store in the refrigerator for up to 2 days; it also freezes well (see Charlie's Tip, page 33). Sprinkle with the remaining 3 tablespoons cilantro before serving.

Fresh
LAYERED SALAD

❧ Serves 12 ❧

1 head iceberg lettuce, shredded

½ cup chopped red onion

½ cup chopped celery

½ cup chopped yellow bell pepper

½ cup cherry tomatoes

1 (12-ounce) package frozen peas (a generous 2 cups), thawed

½ cup mayonnaise

½ cup sour cream

1 tablespoon sugar

1 cup grated sharp yellow cheddar cheese

½ pound bacon, cooked and crumbled

In a large serving bowl, layer the lettuce, followed by the onion, celery, bell peppers, tomatoes, and peas.

In a small bowl, combine the mayonnaise and sour cream and stir well. Spread the mayonnaise mixture evenly on top of the pea layer and sprinkle with the sugar. Sprinkle the cheese and bacon evenly over the top. Cover the salad and refrigerate for at least 4 hours or up to overnight before serving.

CHARLIE'S TIP

We like to serve this beautiful salad in a glass serving bowl so you can see the colorful layers.

Caramel & Sea Salt
BROWNIES

⊸≪ *Makes 32 brownies* ≫⊶

FOR THE BROWNIES

Nonstick baking spray

1 cup (2 sticks) unsalted butter, cut into 1-inch pieces

2½ cups granulated sugar

1½ cups unsweetened cocoa powder

2 teaspoons coarse sea salt

2 teaspoons pure vanilla extract

4 large eggs

⅔ cup all-purpose flour

FOR THE CARAMEL

⅓ cup heavy cream

4 tablespoons (½ stick) unsalted butter, at room temperature

¾ cup packed light brown sugar

Flaky sea salt, such as Maldon

Make the brownies: Preheat the oven to 325°F. Line a 9 x 13-inch baking pan with aluminum foil or parchment paper, leaving a 2-inch overhang on the long sides of the pan. Spray the foil or parchment with baking spray.

In a small saucepan, melt the butter over medium heat. Set aside to cool slightly.

In a medium bowl, whisk together the granulated sugar, cocoa powder, and salt.

While whisking continuously, pour the melted butter into the sugar mixture in a steady stream and whisk until well combined. Stir in the vanilla, then add the eggs one at a time, beating vigorously after each addition to combine. Add the flour and stir until just combined (do not overmix). Scrape the batter into the prepared pan and spread it evenly.

Bake until the top begins to crack and a wooden toothpick or skewer inserted into the center comes out with a few moist crumbs attached, 30 to 40 minutes.

RECIPE CONTINUES

While the brownies are baking, make the caramel: In a heavy-bottomed medium saucepan, combine the heavy cream, butter, brown sugar, and 1½ teaspoons water. Clip a candy thermometer to the side of the pan and heat over medium heat, stirring, until the mixture is smooth, then stop stirring and bring the mixture to a boil. Cook until the thermometer registers 240°F, 5 to 7 minutes.

Remove the brownies from the oven and set the pan on a wire rack. Immediately pour the caramel over the top (be careful, as hot sugar can burn you quite badly) and sprinkle with flaky salt. Let the brownies cool completely in the pan—they will not slice well if they are still warm. Using the overhanging foil or parchment, lift the brownies out of the pan. Transfer them to a cutting board and cut into 32 squares. Store in an airtight container for up to 3 days.

· FOXHUNTING ·
ETIQUETTE

- *If hacking to the meet, never hack through a covert that could potentially be hunted that day. Use the roads as much as possible to avoid moving foxes out of the covert before the hunt.*

English FLAPJACKS

½ cup (1 stick) unsalted butter, plus
    more for the pan

½ cup packed brown sugar

¼ cup golden syrup
    (see Charlie's Tip)

2 cups instant oats

1 cup add-ins, such as currants,
    golden raisins, dried cranberries,
    and/or chocolate chips (see
    Charlie's Tip)

Preheat the oven to 350°F. Lightly grease an 11 x 7-inch baking pan with butter.

In a medium saucepan, melt the butter over medium heat, then stir in the sugar and golden syrup and cook, stirring often, until the sugar has dissolved, 3 to 5 minutes. Remove the mixture from the heat and stir in the oats and add-ins of your choice.

Pour the mixture into the prepared pan, spreading it in an even layer. Bake for 14 to 18 minutes, until the edges are dark golden brown and the center is slightly soft. Remove from the oven and let the bars cool in the pan for 5 minutes.

While still warm (the block will harden and become difficult to cut as it cools), use a sharp knife to carefully cut the block into 50 pieces. Store in an airtight container for up to 3 days.

CHARLIE'S TIP

In the United Kingdom, a "flapjack" is a baked bar traditionally made with oats, butter, and golden syrup (similar to what we know in the United States as a granola bar). A British pantry staple, golden syrup is an amber-colored syrup made from cane sugar, and is slightly thicker than corn syrup. Look for Lyle's Golden Syrup, a popular UK brand. You can also substitute agave nectar or corn syrup if you can't find golden syrup.

For the add-ins, we like to use ¼ cup each of currants, raisins, dried cranberries, and chocolate chips, but use ½ cup each of raisins and cranberries, if you prefer, or even use 1 whole cup chocolate chips!

FOX & HOUND FIRESIDE MEAL

The Perfect Rob Roy 84

Sweet Potato & Chestnut Soup 87

Broccolini with Lemon & Garlic 88

Côte de Boeuf 91

Red Wine Sorbet 92

Bananas Foster Cheesecake 93

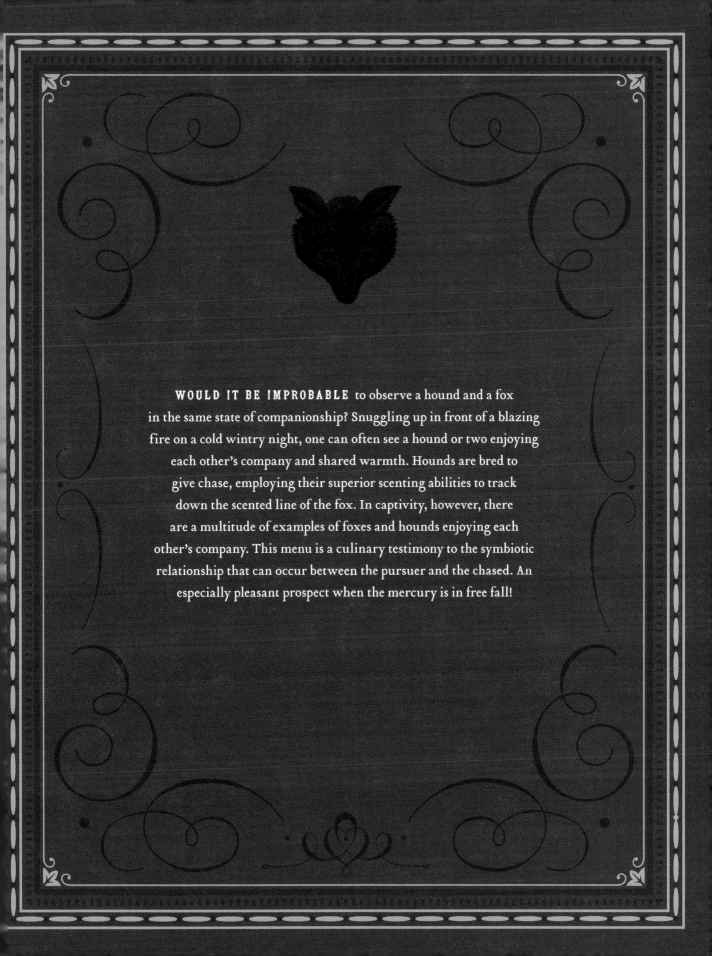

WOULD IT BE IMPROBABLE to observe a hound and a fox in the same state of companionship? Snuggling up in front of a blazing fire on a cold wintry night, one can often see a hound or two enjoying each other's company and shared warmth. Hounds are bred to give chase, employing their superior scenting abilities to track down the scented line of the fox. In captivity, however, there are a multitude of examples of foxes and hounds enjoying each other's company. This menu is a culinary testimony to the symbiotic relationship that can occur between the pursuer and the chased. An especially pleasant prospect when the mercury is in free fall!

The Perfect
ROB ROY

Makes 1 drink

2½ ounces blended Scotch whiskey

1 teaspoon sweet Italian vermouth

1 teaspoon dry French vermouth

Dash of Angostura bitters or
    orange bitters

Handful of ice

Lemon or orange peel, for garnish

Put the whiskey, both vermouths, and the bitters in a cocktail shaker and stir for a minute until well combined. Strain into a double old-fashioned glass filled with ice. Rub the lemon or orange peel over the rim of the glass, then place it in the glass as a garnish and serve.

Master Roy Jackson hunting the Radnor Hounds, 1939

Sweet Potato & Chestnut
SOUP

Serves 6

2 pounds sweet potatoes

2 tablespoons extra-virgin olive oil

2 small yellow onions, thinly sliced

1 cup fresh roasted, canned, or
  jarred peeled chestnuts, chopped
  (see Charlie's Tip, page 88)

½ cup brandy

4 cups chicken broth

1 dried bay leaf

1 teaspoon sea salt

¼ cup crème fraîche

Chopped fresh chives, for garnish

Preheat the oven to 425°F. Line a rimmed baking sheet with parchment paper.

Using a fork, prick the sweet potatoes in several places and place them on the prepared baking sheet. Roast until they are soft and can be pierced easily with a fork, about 1 hour 15 minutes. Remove from the oven. Let cool completely, then peel them and cut them into large chunks. Set aside.

In a large Dutch oven or soup pot, heat the olive oil over medium heat until it shimmers. Add the onions and cook, stirring, for 20 minutes, or until they are soft and just beginning to caramelize. Add ¼ cup water, if needed, to help cook them down. Add the sweet potato chunks, chestnuts, and brandy and simmer for 2 minutes.

Add the broth, bay leaf, and salt. Increase the heat to high and bring the soup to a boil, then reduce the heat to low and simmer for 15 minutes, or until the sweet potatoes start to disintegrate. Remove the soup from the heat and discard the bay leaf.

Working in batches, carefully transfer the soup to a blender and puree until smooth. Ladle the soup into individual serving bowls and top with a dollop of crème fraîche. Garnish with chopped chives and serve.

To roast fresh chestnuts, preheat the oven to 425°F. Using a paring knife, make an X-shaped cut on the round side of each chestnut. Arrange them in a single layer on a rimmed baking sheet and roast for 10 to 20 minutes, until the chestnuts start to open, the skins peel back along the cut side, and the meat is tender when pierced with a knife. While still warm, peel off the outside shell and the papery skin.

BROCCOLINI

WITH LEMON & GARLIC

Serves 4 to 6

1 teaspoon sea salt, plus more to taste

4 bunches Broccolini (about 1½ pounds), stems trimmed

2 tablespoons unsalted butter

2 teaspoons extra-virgin olive oil

2 garlic cloves, minced

1 lemon, cut in half

Freshly ground black pepper

Bring a large pot of water and 1 teaspoon salt to a boil over high heat. Fill a large bowl with ice water and set it nearby. Carefully lower the Broccolini into the boiling water and blanch for a minute or two. Remove the Broccolini, drain well, and immerse it in the ice water to stop it from cooking. Drain again and set aside.

In a large skillet, heat the butter and oil over medium heat until the butter melts. Add the garlic, reduce the heat to low, and cook, stirring continuously, for 1 to 2 minutes, until it just starts to turn golden. Add the blanched Broccolini to the pan and cook for another few minutes until it's heated through. Squeeze the lemon halves over the Broccolini, season with salt and pepper, and serve.

Côte de Boeuf with Broccolini with Lemon & Garlic (page 88)

CÔTE DE BOEUF

❧ Serves 4 to 6 ❧

1 (4-pound) bone-in standing rib roast (see Charlie's Tip), at room temperature

Sea salt and freshly ground black pepper

2 tablespoons unsalted butter

2 tablespoons extra-virgin olive oil

3 tablespoons herb butter

Preheat the oven to 400°F.

Season the rib roast generously with salt and pepper and set aside.

In a large cast-iron skillet, warm the unsalted butter and olive oil over high heat until the butter melts. Add the roast and sear the meat until well browned on each side, 2 to 3 minutes per side.

Transfer the pan to the oven and roast for 20 to 25 minutes, or until the meat reaches an internal temperature of 125°F for rare.

Transfer the meat to a carving board and let rest for 15 minutes.

Carve the meat against the grain, slicing it off the bones. Arrange the slices on a serving platter along with the bones. Top each steak with a dollop of herb butter and serve.

CHARLIE'S TIP

Côte de boeuf, *literally translated as "beef rib," is a thick, bone-in rib steak that is better known as a standing rib roast in the United States (it's also referred to as prime rib—the two terms can be used interchangeably). Prime rib can be sold bone-in or boneless. For this recipe, you want the bones intact, as they lend even more flavor to the already tasty cut of meat.*

Red Wine SORBET

⸻ Serves 4 ⸻

1¼ cups superfine sugar

1 cup boiling water

½ cup fresh orange juice

1 cup light red wine
(see Charlie's Tip)

Place the sugar in a heatproof bowl and pour over the boiling water. Stir until the sugar has completely dissolved. Stir in the orange juice and wine.

Cover and refrigerate for at least 2 hours, or until completely chilled. Pour the chilled mixture into an ice cream maker and churn according to the manufacturer's instructions. The sorbet is done when it has the consistency of soft whipped cream or a very thick but pourable smoothie. Do not overchurn, as it will be more chunky than smooth.

Transfer the sorbet to a freezer-safe container and cover with plastic wrap and a lid. Freeze for at least 4 hours or preferably overnight before serving. Store in the freezer for up to one week.

CHARLIE'S TIP

When cooking with alcohol, it is very important to use wine and spirits only of a quality that you would drink.

Bananas Foster
CHEESECAKE

FOR THE CRUST

Nonstick baking spray

2 cups graham cracker crumbs

¾ cup plus 2 tablespoons packed dark brown sugar

9 tablespoons unsalted butter, melted

1¼ teaspoons pure vanilla extract

3 medium bananas, halved lengthwise

2 tablespoons banana liqueur (crème de banane)

2 tablespoons light rum

FOR THE FILLING

3 (8-ounce) packages cream cheese, at room temperature

½ cup packed light brown sugar

2 large eggs

2 tablespoons sour cream

1½ tablespoons cornstarch

1 teaspoon pure vanilla extract

FOR THE TOPPING

3 tablespoons unsalted butter

2 tablespoons dark brown sugar

3 ripe medium bananas, sliced lengthwise

3 tablespoons banana liqueur (crème de banane)

2 tablespoons light rum

Make the crust: Preheat the oven to 325°F. Position one oven rack in the center position and one in the lowest. On the lowest rack, place a baking pan filled with 1 inch of water. Spray a 9-inch springform pan with baking spray.

In a large bowl, stir together the cracker crumbs, ¼ cup of the brown sugar, 6 tablespoons of the melted butter, and the vanilla until well combined. Press the mixture evenly over the bottom and halfway up the sides of the prepared pan.

RECIPE CONTINUES

In a medium skillet over medium heat, combine the remaining 3 tablespoons melted butter and 2 tablespoons brown sugar and stir until the sugar has dissolved. Add the banana slices and cook for 1 minute. Add the banana liqueur and rum, and cook, stirring often, for 4 minutes. Remove the banana slices from the liquid, reserving the liquid for the filling (you should have a scant ½ cup), and layer the bananas on the bottom of the crust.

Make the filling: In the bowl of a stand mixer fitted with the paddle attachment, beat the cream cheese and light brown sugar on medium-high speed for 2 minutes, or until smooth. Add the eggs one at a time, beating well after each addition. Add the sour cream, cornstarch, vanilla, and the reserved liquid from the banana slices. Beat again on medium until well blended. Pour the filling into the crust over the banana slices.

Place the cake on the middle rack of the oven over the water pan. Bake for 50 to 55 minutes, until the center does not jiggle and the edges are browned. Turn off the oven, wedge the door open with the handle of a wooden spoon, and let the cheesecake cool completely. (Cooling the cake slowly prevents cracks in the top.) Cover the cheesecake with plastic wrap and refrigerate overnight.

Remove the cheesecake from the refrigerator 30 minutes prior to serving.

Meanwhile, make the topping: In a medium skillet, melt the butter over medium-high heat. Add the sugar and stir until the sugar has dissolved. Add the banana pieces and cook, stirring, for about 1 minute. Add the banana liqueur and light rum, and cook, stirring often, for 3 to 4 minutes. Remove from the heat.

To serve, run a sharp knife between the cake and the sides of the pan to loosen the cake. Release the sides of the springform pan and remove the ring. Place the cheesecake on a serving platter and spoon the topping over the top.

FULL OF THE MOON
ROUNDTABLE

Rosemary Maple Bourbon Sour 98

Cocoa Espresso Cardamom Almonds 101

Seared Sesame Tuna Bites 102

Clementines, Cabbage & Romaine Salad 104

Coq au Vin 105

Party Potatoes 108

Dark Chocolate Hazelnut Tart 111

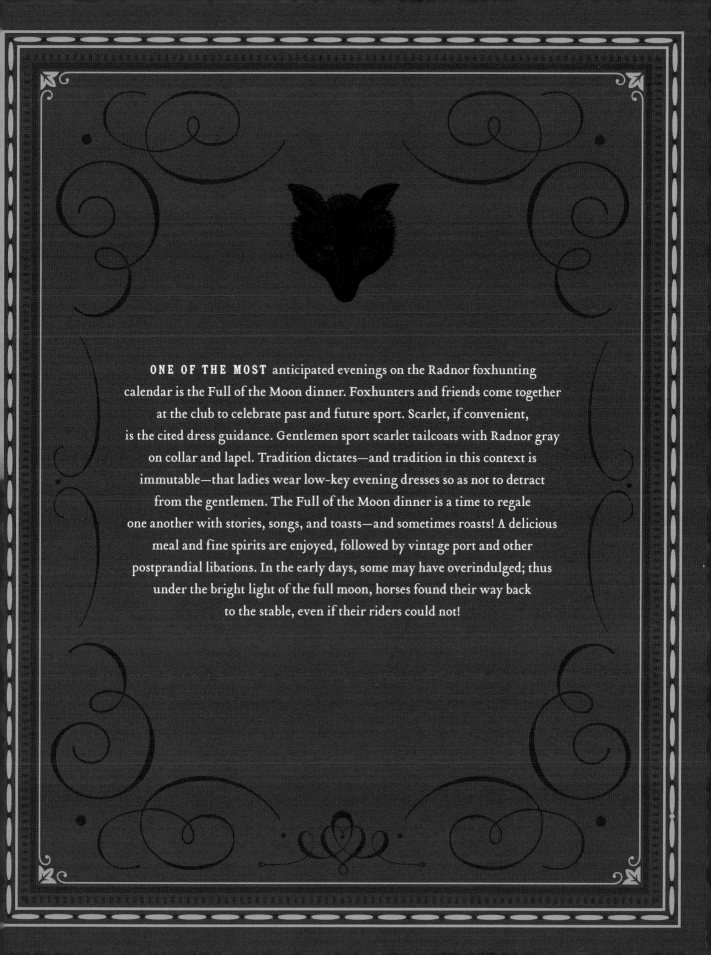

ONE OF THE MOST anticipated evenings on the Radnor foxhunting
calendar is the Full of the Moon dinner. Foxhunters and friends come together
at the club to celebrate past and future sport. Scarlet, if convenient,
is the cited dress guidance. Gentlemen sport scarlet tailcoats with Radnor gray
on collar and lapel. Tradition dictates—and tradition in this context is
immutable—that ladies wear low-key evening dresses so as not to detract
from the gentlemen. The Full of the Moon dinner is a time to regale
one another with stories, songs, and toasts—and sometimes roasts! A delicious
meal and fine spirits are enjoyed, followed by vintage port and other
postprandial libations. In the early days, some may have overindulged; thus
under the bright light of the full moon, horses found their way back
to the stable, even if their riders could not!

Rosemary Maple
BOURBON SOUR

~ Makes 1 drink ~

1 large sprig fresh rosemary, plus a small sprig for garnish

1 ounce fresh lemon juice

2 ounces bourbon

½ ounce dark amber pure maple syrup

2 handfuls of ice

Combine the large rosemary sprig and the lemon juice in a cocktail shaker and crush with a muddler (alternatively, you can crush the rosemary with your hand and then add to the shaker). Let stand for at least 30 minutes for the flavors to develop (this step can be skipped if you're short on time).

Add the bourbon, maple syrup, and a handful of ice and shake vigorously for 15 seconds.

Fill a lowball or old-fashioned glass with the remaining ice and strain the mixture into it. Garnish with the small rosemary sprig. Serve immediately.

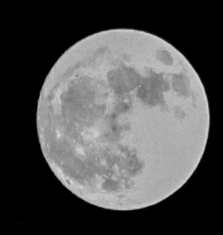

*Rosemary Maple Bourbon Sour
(page 98) with Cocoa Espresso
Cardamom Almonds*

Cocoa Espresso Cardamom
ALMONDS

꙰ *Makes 3 cups* ꙰

½ cup sugar

2 tablespoons unsweetened cocoa
powder

2 teaspoons instant espresso powder

1½ teaspoons ground cardamom

½ teaspoon sea salt

1 large egg white

1 tablespoon vanilla bean paste (see
Charlie's Tip)

3 cups raw almonds (about 1 pound)

Preheat the oven to 275°F. Line a rimmed baking sheet with parchment paper.

In a small bowl, combine the sugar, cocoa powder, espresso powder, cardamom, and salt.
Set aside.

In a large bowl, whisk together the egg white and vanilla bean paste until frothy. Add
the almonds and stir to coat them with the egg white mixture. Pour the sugar-cocoa
mixture over the almonds and toss gently until they are evenly coated.

Transfer the almonds to the prepared baking sheet and spread them into an even layer.
Bake for 40 minutes, or until aromatic, stirring every 10 to 15 minutes. Watch them
carefully so they do not burn. Transfer the baking sheet to a wire rack and let the
almonds cool completely. Once cooled, break any clusters into individual almonds and
serve. Store in an airtight container for up to 2 weeks or in the freezer for up to 3 months.

CHARLIE'S
TIP

*We love the heady, rich scent of Nielsen-Massey Madagascar Bourbon
Pure Vanilla Bean Paste, and it is our preferred brand to use for this recipe. You can also
substitute 1 tablespoon pure vanilla extract or the seeds from 1 vanilla bean.*

Seared
SESAME TUNA BITES

꙰ Makes 36 bites ꙰

½ cup white sesame seeds

½ cup black sesame seeds

2 tablespoons toasted sesame oil

1 tablespoon vegetable oil

1¼ pounds fresh tuna steaks,
  cut 1-inch thick, rinsed and
  patted dry

Sea salt and freshly ground
  black pepper

Wasabi mayonnaise or soy sauce,
  for serving

Wasabi peas (optional), for garnish

Combine the sesame seeds in a pie pan or on a large plate and set aside. In a small bowl, stir together the oils. Season the tuna with salt and pepper. Using a pastry brush, coat each of the steaks with the oil mixture, then dip them in the sesame seeds, thoroughly coating both sides.

Heat a large skillet over medium-high heat. When it's piping hot, add the tuna steaks. Cook for 1 minute, then flip and cook for another minute.

Remove the steaks from the pan and allow them to rest for 5 minutes. Using a very sharp knife, cut the tuna into bite-size chunks.

To serve, arrange the tuna pieces on a platter and drizzle with wasabi mayonnaise, or serve with soy sauce alongside. Garnish with wasabi peas, if desired.

CHARLIE'S TIP

One of our favorite ways to serve these sesame bites is with decorative toothpicks (see opposite). Just pop one into each bite and voilà—your appetizer just got a little prettier.

Clementines, Cabbage & Romaine
SALAD

※ Serves 6 ※

FOR THE SALAD

1 small head napa cabbage, thinly
    sliced

1 small head romaine lettuce,
    chopped

1 cup chopped celery

3 tablespoons minced fresh parsley

6 scallions, thinly sliced

6 clementines, peeled, separated, and
    the membrane removed

¾ cup slivered almonds, toasted
    (see Charlie's Tip, page 34)

FOR THE DRESSING

6 tablespoons white balsamic
    vinegar

¼ cup sugar

1½ teaspoons sea salt

¾ teaspoon Tabasco sauce

¾ cup extra-virgin olive oil

Make the salad: In a large bowl, place all the ingredients for the salad and toss to combine. Refrigerate until ready to serve.

Make the dressing: In a small bowl, whisk together the vinegar, sugar, salt, and Tabasco until the salt and sugar have dissolved. While whisking, drizzle in the oil and whisk until emulsified.

Just before serving, drizzle some of the dressing over the salad and toss until lightly and evenly coated. You may not use all the dressing, depending on your taste preference. Refrigerate any leftover dressing in an airtight container for up to 2 weeks.

COQ AU VIN

6 whole skin-on chicken legs
(see Charlie's Tip, page 107)

3 teaspoons sea salt, plus more to
taste

Freshly ground black pepper

3 tablespoons extra-virgin olive oil

3 carrots, peeled and chopped

1 yellow onion, chopped

4 cups dry red wine (about one
750 ml bottle), such as Burgundy
or Pinot Noir

½ cup tomato paste

4 cups chicken broth

Bouquet garni: 12 sprigs fresh thyme
and 6 sprigs fresh rosemary
(see Charlie's Tip, page 107)

1 pound cremini mushrooms,
cleaned and chopped (about
8 cups)

Preheat the oven to 350°F. Position a rack in the lower third of the oven, making sure the Dutch oven or pot you'll be using, including its lid, fits comfortably inside.

Season the chicken thoroughly with 1½ teaspoons of the salt and pepper to taste. In a large Dutch oven or ovenproof pot with a lid, heat 2 tablespoons of the olive oil over medium-high heat until it starts to shimmer. Working in batches, add the chicken and cook until browned on both sides, 5 to 6 minutes per side. Using tongs, transfer the chicken to a plate and set aside.

Add the carrots and onion to the same pot and cook over medium-high heat until the onion is translucent and the carrots have softened, 8 to 10 minutes. Whisk in 1 cup of the wine, the tomato paste, and remaining 1½ teaspoons salt. Bring the mixture to a simmer and cook for 3 minutes. Add the remaining 3 cups wine and bring it to a boil. Cook, uncovered, until the wine has reduced by half, 15 to 20 minutes.

Return the chicken to the pot. Pour in the broth and add the bouquet garni. Bring the mixture back to a boil, then cover and transfer to the oven. Braise until the chicken is very tender, about 1 hour 15 minutes.

RECIPE CONTINUES

Coq au Vin with Party Potatoes (page 108); wine from White Horse Winery owned by the Vinton family, Radnor Hunt members

COQ AU VIN
CONTINUED

Meanwhile, in a large pot, heat the remaining 1 tablespoon olive oil over medium heat until it just starts to shimmer. Add the mushrooms, sprinkle with a few pinches of salt, and cook, stirring, until they just start to soften, about 5 minutes. Remove from the heat.

When the chicken is done cooking, transfer the whole chicken from the braising pot, leaving the braising liquid in the pot, to the pot with the mushrooms and keep warm over low heat.

Bring the braising liquid to a simmer over medium-high heat and cook for 20 minutes, or until the liquid has reduced by one-third. Discard the bouquet garni. Pour the sauce over the mushrooms and chicken. Season with salt and pepper. Serve immediately, or see Charlie's Tip for reheating information.

CHARLIE'S TIP

For this recipe, we use whole chicken legs, which are the drumstick-thigh combination and are also referred to as chicken leg quarters. We also make a "bouquet garni," which is simply aromatics tied together in a bundle using unwaxed kitchen string, which makes them easy to remove after cooking, instead of having to fish around for loose stems.

Coq au vin can be made in advance, and it is actually better made at least a day ahead so the flavors can meld and deepen. Allow the dish to cool completely, then cover and refrigerate for up to 2 days. To reheat, spoon off any fat that has accumulated, and heat the coq au vin, covered, in a preheated 350°F oven for 30 minutes, or until the chicken is heated through.

Party POTATOES

※ Serves 6 ※

1 tablespoon extra-virgin olive oil, plus more for the baking dish

2½ pounds Yukon Gold potatoes, peeled and cut into 1-inch pieces

¼ pound sweet potatoes, peeled and cut into 1-inch pieces

3 teaspoons sea salt

4 ounces cream cheese, at room temperature and cut into 1-inch pieces (see Charlie's Tip)

3 tablespoons unsalted butter, melted

2 tablespoons whole milk

Freshly ground black pepper

Preheat the oven to 400°F. Lightly oil a 3-quart baking dish.

Put the Yukon Gold and sweet potatoes in a large pot, fill with water to cover, add 2 teaspoons of the salt, and bring to a boil over high heat. Reduce the heat to medium and simmer for 25 minutes, or until the potatoes are fork-tender. Drain well.

Pass the cooked potatoes through a ricer into a large bowl (or mash them by hand). Do not overmix. Using a wooden spoon, stir in the cheese, butter, milk, and olive oil. You can add a little more milk and/or oil if you like your potatoes a little thinner. Season with the remaining 1 teaspoon sea salt and pepper to taste.

Spread the potatoes in the prepared baking dish. Bake for about 35 minutes, or until heated through and the top is lightly golden. Remove from the oven and serve.

CHARLIE'S TIP

You can use any soft cheese, such as mascarpone, or even thick cream, such as crème fraîche, in this recipe. We also like to add a handful of fresh herbs, such as chopped rosemary or tarragon, chopped prosciutto or bacon, or even sun-dried tomatoes to the potatoes.

The potatoes can be prepared up to 2 days in advance. After baking, cool to room temperature, then cover and refrigerate. To reheat, bring the potatoes to room temperature, cover with aluminum foil, and bake in a preheated 350°F oven for 35 minutes, or until heated through.

· FOXHUNTING ·
ETIQUETTE

- *Delay jumping a fence if there is danger of harming a hound.*

- *When approaching a jump, avoid crossing in front of another of the field. When you are headed for a certain panel, jump that one.*

- *Give a person "room to fall." Don't crowd going into a fence.*

- *If your horse refuses a fence, go to the rear of the field to try again.*

Dark Chocolate
HAZELNUT TART

⊰ Makes one 9-inch tart ⊱

FOR THE CRUST

1½ cups gingersnap cookie crumbs

6 tablespoons (¾ stick) unsalted
butter, melted

¼ teaspoon fine sea salt

FOR THE FILLING

1 cup hazelnuts, coarsely chopped

1 cup heavy cream

10 ounces high-quality bittersweet
chocolate, finely chopped

½ cup chocolate-hazelnut spread,
such as Nutella, at room
temperature

½ teaspoon coarse sea salt

Preheat the oven to 350°F. Position a rack in the lower third of the oven.

Make the crust: In a medium bowl, stir together the gingersnap crumbs, butter, and salt. Press the mixture evenly over the bottom of a 9-inch springform pan. Bake the crust for 7 minutes, then transfer to a wire rack and let cool completely in the pan.

Make the filling: While the crust bakes, put the hazelnuts in a baking dish and toast in the oven, stirring once, for 3 to 5 minutes, until they just start to turn golden. Transfer the pan to the rack next to the crust and let cool.

In a medium saucepan, bring the cream to a boil over medium-high heat, then remove it from the heat and add the chocolate. Let sit for 5 minutes, then whisk until the mixture is completely smooth and combined. Whisk in the chocolate-hazelnut spread. Stir in the toasted nuts, setting aside a tablespoon for garnish, and the coarse sea salt.

Pour the filling into the cooled crust and freeze until just set, about 25 minutes (do not let the tart fully freeze). Transfer the tart to the refrigerator until ready to serve.

Bring the tart to room temperature for about 20 minutes before serving. Garnish with the reserved chopped hazelnuts. Slice and serve.

Plantation Field, Cheshire Land Preservation Fund

DOGS' DINNER

Sun-Dried Tomato & Caper Tapenade 116

Golden Mushroom Soup 119

Red Wine–Braised Short Ribs 122

Corn & Saffron Risotto 124

Zucchini Cakes 125

White Russian Cocktail 126

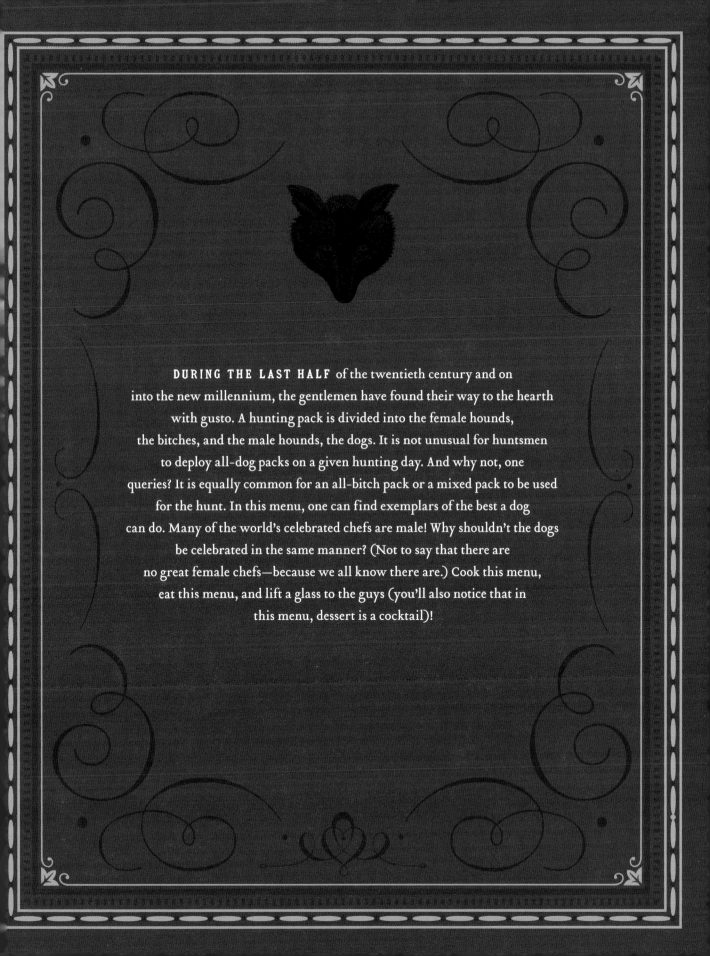

DURING THE LAST HALF of the twentieth century and on
into the new millennium, the gentlemen have found their way to the hearth
with gusto. A hunting pack is divided into the female hounds,
the bitches, and the male hounds, the dogs. It is not unusual for huntsmen
to deploy all-dog packs on a given hunting day. And why not, one
queries? It is equally common for an all-bitch pack or a mixed pack to be used
for the hunt. In this menu, one can find exemplars of the best a dog
can do. Many of the world's celebrated chefs are male! Why shouldn't the dogs
be celebrated in the same manner? (Not to say that there are
no great female chefs—because we all know there are.) Cook this menu,
eat this menu, and lift a glass to the guys (you'll also notice that in
this menu, dessert is a cocktail)!

Sun-Dried Tomato & Caper TAPENADE

❈ Makes about 2 cups ❈

6 ounces sun-dried tomatoes (about 2 cups), not oil-packed, chopped

Boiling water

2 garlic cloves

2 to 3 tablespoons extra-virgin olive oil

1 tablespoon tomato paste

½ cup capers, drained, plus a few for garnish

Sea salt and freshly ground black pepper

Baguette slices, for serving

Place the sun-dried tomatoes in a heatproof bowl and add boiling water to cover. Soak for 15 minutes, or until soft. Drain well, reserving ¼ cup of the soaking liquid.

In a food processor, combine the reconstituted sun-dried tomatoes and garlic and puree until smooth. With the motor running, add 2 tablespoons of the oil and 2 tablespoons of the reserved soaking liquid through the feed tube and process until smooth, adding more of the oil and soaking liquid as needed. Add the tomato paste and process to combine. Add the capers and season with salt and pepper. Puree until combined. The dip should maintain some chunks and be thickish.

The tapenade is best if you refrigerate it for a few hours so the flavors can blend. Bring it to room temperature before serving and garnish with extra capers. Serve with baguette slices. Store in an airtight container in the refrigerator for up to 1 week.

· FOXHUNTING ·
ETIQUETTE

- *Juniors, new members, green horses, and guests are expected to ride in the rear of the field.*

Golden MUSHROOM SOUP

⁓⁂ Serves 4 to 6 ⁂⁓

½ cup (1 stick) unsalted butter

4 medium shallots, chopped (about 1 cup)

16 cups sliced white mushrooms (about 4 pounds)

4 cups chicken broth

3 cups dry white wine, such as Sauvignon Blanc, plus more if needed

Sea salt and freshly ground black pepper

Sour cream, for serving

Thinly sliced scallions, for serving

In a large Dutch oven or pot, melt the butter over medium heat. Add the shallots and cook, stirring occasionally, for 5 minutes, or until they start to soften. Add the mushrooms and cook for 5 minutes more, or until they begin to lightly brown. Add the broth and wine and bring the mixture to a boil. Reduce the heat to low and simmer, stirring occasionally, for 1 hour, or until the broth becomes rich and has reduced by about 1 cup. If the soup reduces down too much, add more wine. Season with salt and pepper.

Ladle into bowls. Serve topped with a dollop of sour cream and sprinkled with a few scallions.

· FOXHUNTING ·
ETIQUETTE

- *If branches or other obstructions are on the path and are movable by hand, dismount and move the debris if time allows.*

- *Brush by or duck under branches. DO NOT hold them, as they will snap back to hit the person behind you.*

Brandywine Red Clay Alliance

Red Wine–Braised
SHORT RIBS

⊰⊱ Serves 4 ⊰⊱

2 tablespoons extra-virgin olive oil

4 boneless short ribs, about 8 ounces each

2 yellow onions, chopped

4 celery stalks, chopped

2 carrots, peeled and cut into large dice

6 garlic cloves, minced

1 tablespoon tomato paste

2½ quarts beef broth

2 cups dry red wine

Preheat the oven to 350°F. Position a rack in the lower third of the oven.

In a Dutch oven or large ovenproof pot with a lid, heat the olive oil over high heat until it shimmers. Working in batches, using tongs, brown the short ribs on all sides, 3 to 5 minutes per side, and transfer them to a plate. Set aside.

Reduce the heat to medium. Add the onions, celery, carrots, and garlic and cook, stirring, for 5 minutes. Add the tomato paste, stirring well to coat the vegetables, and cook for 3 minutes more. Add the broth and wine, increase the heat to medium-high, and bring the mixture to a simmer. Whisk until the tomato paste is completely incorporated. Return the ribs to the pot, along with any accumulated juices from the plate, and cover. Bake for 2 hours 30 minutes. The meat should be fork-tender.

To serve, transfer the short ribs to a serving platter. Skim any fat off the sauce in the pot and transfer the sauce to a blender. Puree on high until smooth and spoon over the ribs before serving.

Red Wine–Braised Short Ribs with
Corn & Saffron Risotto (page 124)

Corn & Saffron
RISOTTO

Serves 4

4¼ cups chicken broth

½ teaspoon saffron threads

½ cup (1 stick) unsalted butter

4 cups fresh sweet corn kernels (cut from about 4 medium ears)

1 carrot, peeled and chopped

¼ teaspoon sea salt

¼ teaspoon freshly ground black pepper

3 shallots, minced

1 tablespoon extra-virgin olive oil

1 cup Arborio rice

½ cup white wine or vegetable broth

2 tablespoons heavy cream

¼ cup chopped parsley

In a medium pot, combine 4 cups of the broth and the saffron. Bring the liquid to a simmer over medium heat, then cover and reduce the heat to the lowest setting to keep the broth warm.

In a large pot, melt 3 tablespoons of the butter over medium heat. Add the corn and carrot and sprinkle with the salt and pepper. Stir to combine. Pour in the remaining ¼ cup broth and cook, stirring occasionally, for 5 to 8 minutes, or until the carrot is tender. Remove the corn from the pot with a slotted spoon and set aside. Discard any remaining liquid in the pan.

In the same pot, melt 3 tablespoons of the butter over medium heat. Add the shallots and cook for 8 minutes, or until softened. Add the olive oil and rice, stirring well to coat, and cook, stirring occasionally, for 2 to 3 minutes. Reduce the heat and pour in the wine. Cook, stirring continuously, until all the liquid has been absorbed. Add the warm broth, ½ cup at a time, stirring continuously and allowing the liquid to be absorbed after each addition before adding the next, just until the mixture becomes creamy and the rice is almost tender, about 20 minutes.

Stir in the cream, the corn, and the remaining 2 tablespoons butter. Cook, stirring, until heated through. Sprinkle with the parsley and serve immediately.

ZUCCHINI CAKES

≋ Serves 4 ≋

1½ cups coarsely grated zucchini (from about 1 large zucchini)

¼ teaspoon sea salt

½ cup breadcrumbs (see Charlie's Tip)

1 large egg

1 scallion, white part only, thinly sliced

2 tablespoons diced red bell pepper

¾ teaspoon Old Bay seasoning

½ teaspoon Dijon mustard

1½ teaspoons mayonnaise

Pinch of red pepper flakes

1 tablespoon extra-virgin olive oil

1 tablespoon unsalted butter

Sour cream, for serving (optional)

Line a rimmed baking sheet with parchment paper.

Place the grated zucchini in a colander set over a bowl or in the sink. Sprinkle lightly with salt and let stand for 30 minutes, then press with paper towels to remove as much liquid from the zucchini as possible (the zucchini should be fairly dry and measure about 1 cup).

In a bowl, combine the drained zucchini, breadcrumbs, egg, scallion, bell pepper, Old Bay, Dijon, mayonnaise, and red pepper flakes and stir well. Using your hands, form the mixture into 8 patties and place them on the prepared baking sheet.

In a large skillet, heat the olive oil and butter over medium-high heat until the butter has melted. Working in batches, if needed, to avoid crowding the pan, use a spatula to gently slide the patties into the pan and cook for 3 minutes per side, or until golden on both sides. Drain on paper towels. Serve with a dollop of sour cream, if desired.

CHARLIE'S TIP

Homemade breadcrumbs are a cinch to make. Simply tear stale bread into a few small pieces, place in a food processor, and pulse several times until you have fine crumbs. If you don't have stale bread, you can lightly toast a few slices, then make crumbs. We especially love making sourdough breadcrumbs.

WHITE RUSSIAN
Cocktail

※ *Makes 1 drink* ※

Handful of ice

1½ ounces vodka

1 ounce coffee liqueur, store-bought (such as Tia Maria) or homemade (recipe follows)

1 ounce heavy cream

Fill a lowball or old-fashioned glass with ice. Pour in the vodka and coffee liqueur, and top with the cream. Leave layered or stir to combine before serving.

HOMEMADE COFFEE LIQUEUR

Makes about 2 cups

1 vanilla bean

¾ cup ground dark coffee (regular or decaffeinated)

1 cup vodka

¼ cup agave nectar, plus more as needed

¼ cup pure maple syrup, plus more as needed

In a small saucepan, combine 1½ cups water and the vanilla bean and bring the water to a boil over high heat. Remove the pan from the heat. Remove the vanilla bean and set it aside. Add the coffee to the water in the pan and let steep for 5 minutes.

Strain the coffee through a fine-mesh sieve lined with a coffee filter into a medium heatproof bowl. If you see any grounds in the strained coffee, strain the mixture again.

Add the reserved vanilla bean, vodka, agave, and maple syrup to the coffee. Stir well. Let cool completely. Taste and add more agave or maple syrup, if desired. Transfer the mixture to a bottle or mason jar, seal tightly, and refrigerate for at least 3 days before using, and up to 2 months.

The three main elements of this rich cocktail—coffee, sugar, and cream—are used in many beloved desserts. With this menu, we like to serve this decadent drink as a sweet ending to the meal.

SUPPER AT THE PUB

Apple Cider Rumtini 130

Blue Cheese Pecans 133

Beer Cheese 134

Scotch Eggs 137

Truffle Pizza 138

Sausage Shepherd's Pie 141

Venison Chili 143

Calypso Turkey Sliders 144

Green Bean Fries 146

Chocolate Bourbon Pecan Bread Pudding 149

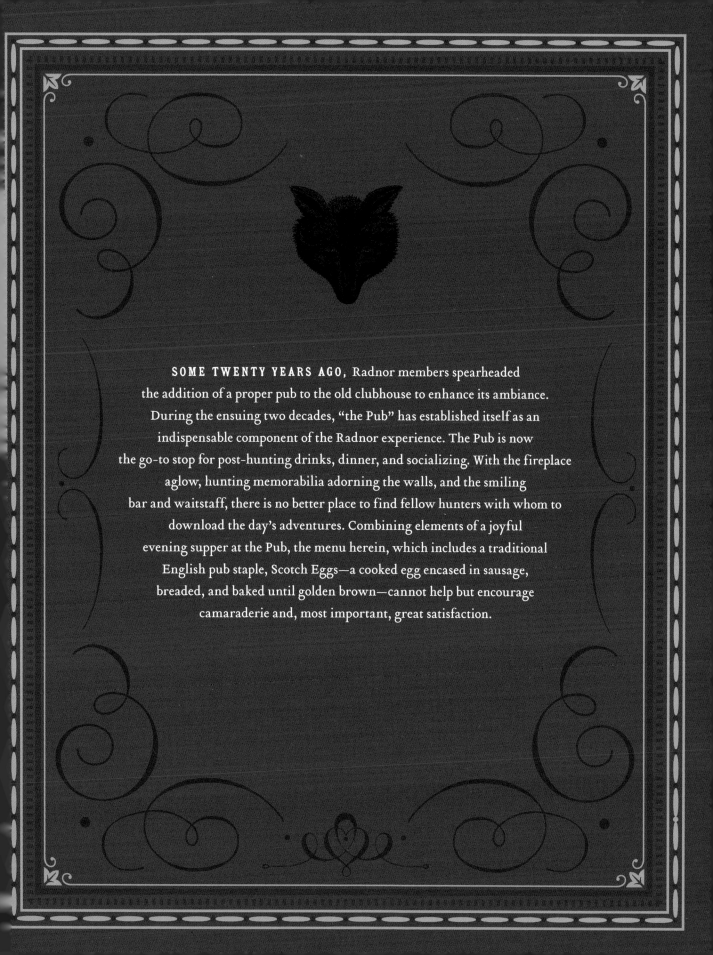

SOME TWENTY YEARS AGO, Radnor members spearheaded
the addition of a proper pub to the old clubhouse to enhance its ambiance.
During the ensuing two decades, "the Pub" has established itself as an
indispensable component of the Radnor experience. The Pub is now
the go-to stop for post-hunting drinks, dinner, and socializing. With the fireplace
aglow, hunting memorabilia adorning the walls, and the smiling
bar and waitstaff, there is no better place to find fellow hunters with whom to
download the day's adventures. Combining elements of a joyful
evening supper at the Pub, the menu herein, which includes a traditional
English pub staple, Scotch Eggs—a cooked egg encased in sausage,
breaded, and baked until golden brown—cannot help but encourage
camaraderie and, most important, great satisfaction.

Apple Cider RUMTINI

⚶ *Makes 1 drink* ⚶

½ teaspoon ground cinnamon

½ teaspoon sugar

3½ ounces apple cider

2 ounces amber rum

1 teaspoon pure maple syrup

Handful of ice

Combine the cinnamon and sugar on a small plate. On another small plate, pour a thin layer of water. Dip the rim of a martini glass in the water and then in the cinnamon-sugar mixture to coat. Set aside.

In a cocktail shaker, combine the apple cider, rum, maple syrup, and ice. Shake well to combine. Strain into the prepared glass and serve.

CHARLIE'S TIP

To serve a crowd, increase the quantities of each ingredient accordingly, except the ice, and mix in a pitcher. This cocktail can be made a few hours in advance and kept in the refrigerator until it's time to serve. The glasses can be rimmed in advance, too. When you're ready to serve, fill a large mason jar three-quarters full with ice and pour 10 to 12 ounces of the pre-mixed cocktail into the jar. Shake as you normally would and strain to serve, dividing the mixture among 3 or 4 glasses.

Radnor Hunt Pub

Apple Cider Rumtini (page 130)
with Blue Cheese Pecans

Blue Cheese
PECANS

⁓❋ Makes 3 cups ❋⁓

2 tablespoons unsalted butter

½ cup crumbled blue cheese (about 2½ ounces; see Charlie's Tip)

3 cups raw pecan halves (about 12 ounces)

Dash of cayenne pepper (optional)

Preheat the oven to 350°F. Line a large baking sheet with parchment paper.

In a small pot, combine the butter and blue cheese. Heat over medium heat, stirring continuously, until melted, well blended, and smooth. Add the pecans and toss to coat. If desired, add the cayenne and toss again.

Spread the pecans in a single layer on the prepared baking sheet and bake for about 10 minutes, or until toasted and fragrant. Watch them carefully, as they burn fast.

Transfer the pan to a wire rack and let the nuts cool completely before serving. Store in an airtight container in the refrigerator for up to 2 weeks or in the freezer for up to 3 months.

CHARLIE'S TIP

This recipe can easily be doubled—just be sure to use two separate baking sheets to give the nuts proper real estate.

If you like a strong blue cheese flavor, ask your cheesemonger for an intense blue cheese.

BEER CHEESE

Makes 2½ cups

1 pound good-quality sharp cheddar cheese, grated

1 large garlic clove

2 teaspoons Worcestershire sauce

¼ teaspoon dry mustard

¼ teaspoon freshly ground black pepper

⅛ to ¼ teaspoon cayenne pepper

¾ cup amber or lager beer

Small pretzels or crackers, for serving

In a food processor, combine the cheese, garlic, Worcestershire, mustard, black pepper, and cayenne and pulse to combine. With the motor running, slowly pour the beer in through the feed tube and process until the mixture is smooth.

Transfer the beer cheese to a serving bowl and cover with plastic wrap. Refrigerate for at least 3 hours or up to overnight (the longer it sits, the more the flavors will develop). Bring it to room temperature before serving. Serve with pretzels or crackers.

CHARLIE'S TIP

For a bolder taste, add 3 tablespoons prepared horseradish.

This cheese can be made up to several days in advance and stored in the refrigerator.

SCOTCH EGGS

Nonstick cooking spray

14 large eggs

2 cups all-purpose flour

2 cups Italian-style seasoned
    breadcrumbs

2 pounds sweet Italian sausage

Sea salt and freshly ground pepper

A few handfuls of arugula, for
    serving

Sliced radishes, for serving

Spicy mustard, for serving

Preheat the oven to 325°F. Spray two rimmed baking sheets with cooking spray.

Place 12 of the eggs in a single layer in the bottom of a large pot and add enough water to cover them by 2 inches. Bring the water to a boil over high heat, then remove the pot from the heat and cover. Allow the eggs to sit in the water for 10 minutes. Meanwhile, fill a large bowl with ice and water and set it nearby. After the eggs have rested in the water, drain them and place them in the ice water to cool for 5 minutes. Drain them again, gently crack and peel them, and set aside.

Crack the remaining 2 raw eggs into a wide, shallow bowl and whisk lightly. Place the flour in a second wide, shallow bowl and the breadcrumbs in a third.

Divide the sausage into 12 portions. Roll each portion into a ball and, using the palm of your hand, flatten each ball.

Roll a hard-boiled egg in the flour, then gently form a flattened sausage patty around the egg, completely encasing the egg. Set aside on a large plate. Repeat with the remaining hard-boiled eggs and sausage.

Roll a sausage-encased egg in the flour, shaking off the excess, then dip it in the beaten eggs and immediately roll it in the breadcrumbs to coat. Place the breaded ball on the prepared baking sheet and repeat to bread the remaining sausage eggs.

Bake for 35 to 45 minutes, until golden brown. Transfer the baking sheets to wire racks and let the eggs cool for 15 minutes.

Season the eggs with salt and pepper. Arrange a bed of arugula with sliced radishes on a platter. Slice each egg in half, set them on the platter, and serve immediately, with mustard passed alongside.

TRUFFLE PIZZA

Serves 6

FOR THE DOUGH

⅓ cup warm water

1 teaspoon sugar

1 teaspoon active dry yeast

1 cup all-purpose flour

1 teaspoon sea salt

1 tablespoon extra-virgin olive oil, plus more for the bowl

A few tablespoons cornmeal

FOR THE TOPPING

3 tablespoons garlic oil

3 tablespoons truffle oil

1 pound fresh mozzarella cheese, grated

1½ cups coarsely grated Parmesan cheese (about 6 ounces)

3 to 4 tablespoons chopped truffles in oil

Sea salt and/or truffle salt

Freshly ground black pepper

Make the dough: In a small bowl, whisk together the warm water, sugar, and yeast. Let stand for 10 minutes, or until it becomes frothy.

In a large bowl, combine the flour and sea salt. Add the yeast mixture and the olive oil and stir until fully combined.

Grease a large bowl with olive oil. On a floured surface, knead the dough for 5 minutes, then shape the dough into a ball. Place the dough in the greased bowl, cover it with a dish towel, and let it rise in a warm place for 1 to 2 hours, until it has doubled in size.

Meanwhile, place a pizza stone in the oven and preheat the oven to 450°F. Allow the stone to preheat for 20 minutes.

Turn the dough out onto a floured surface and roll it into a 12-inch round.

Sprinkle a pizza peel (or rimless cookie sheet) with cornmeal. Put the dough round on the peel (or cookie sheet) and brush it liberally with the garlic oil and truffle oil. Sprinkle evenly with the mozzarella and Parmesan, then the chopped truffles. Slide the assembled pizza gently onto the stone. Bake for 10 minutes, or until the crust is golden and the cheeses just start to bubble.

Remove the pizza from the oven. Season with sea salt and/or truffle salt and pepper. Serve immediately.

Sausage
SHEPHERD'S PIE

Serves 6

1 pound butternut squash, peeled, seeded, and cut into 2-inch-long pieces (about 1½ cups)

1½ pounds sweet potatoes, peeled and cut into 2-inch pieces (about 5 cups)

1 medium russet potato, peeled and cut into 2-inch pieces (about 1 cup)

1 teaspoon sea salt, plus more to taste

2 tablespoons unsalted butter, plus more for the pan

2 tablespoons pure maple syrup

Freshly ground black pepper

1½ pounds mixed hot and sweet Italian sausage, casings removed

2 yellow onions, chopped (about 2 cups)

3 garlic cloves, minced

¾ cup cooked peas

¾ cup cooked corn kernels

⅓ cup heavy cream

1 large egg, lightly beaten

1½ teaspoons curry powder

½ teaspoon ground coriander

6 drops of hot sauce

In a large pot, combine the squash, sweet potatoes, and russet potatoes, add water to cover and the salt, and bring to a boil over high heat. Reduce the heat to medium and simmer for 25 minutes, or until the potatoes and squash are fork-tender. Drain well.

Transfer the potatoes and squash to a large bowl. Add the butter and maple syrup and mash with a potato masher until smooth. Season generously with salt and pepper.

Preheat the oven to 350°F. Lightly butter an 8-inch square glass or ceramic baking dish.

In a large skillet, cook the sausage over medium-high heat, breaking it up with the back of a spoon and stirring occasionally, until browned and heated through. Using a slotted spoon, transfer the sausage to a large bowl. Discard all but 1 tablespoon of the rendered fat from the skillet.

RECIPE CONTINUES

SAUSAGE SHEPHERD'S PIE
CONTINUED

Add the onions and garlic to the rendered fat and cook over medium-high heat for 7 minutes, or until the onions are tender and the garlic just starts to turn golden. Transfer the onion mixture to the bowl with the sausage. Season with salt and pepper. Let cool for 10 minutes, or until no longer hot to the touch, then stir in the peas, corn, cream, egg, curry powder, coriander, and hot sauce.

Transfer the sausage mixture to the prepared baking dish. Spoon the squash-potato mixture evenly over the top and smooth it with a rubber spatula or the back of a spoon. Bake for 45 minutes, or until heated through and the topping just begins to brown around the edges. Remove from the oven and let stand for 5 minutes before serving.

CHARLIE'S TIP

This Sausage Shepherd's Pie can be assembled 1 day in advance.
Cover and refrigerate the unbaked pie. When ready to serve, bake the pie straight
from the refrigerator, but add an extra 15 minutes to the baking time.

VENISON CHILI

Serves 8

2 tablespoons extra-virgin olive oil

2 pounds ground venison

2 yellow onions, diced

4 garlic cloves, minced

1 green bell pepper, cut into thin, 1½-inch-long strips

1 red bell pepper, cut into thin, 1½-inch-long strips

2 poblano peppers, cut into thin, 1½-inch-long strips

2 tablespoons chili powder

1 tablespoon ancho chile powder

1 tablespoon ground cumin

2 teaspoons onion powder

2 teaspoons paprika

1½ teaspoons dried oregano

¾ teaspoon dried thyme

½ teaspoon sea salt, plus more to taste

1 (15½-ounce) can kidney beans, drained and rinsed

1 (28-ounce) can crushed tomatoes

1 cup dry red wine

2 tablespoons red wine vinegar

Shredded sharp cheddar cheese, for serving

Sour cream, for serving

Sliced scallions, for garnish

In a Dutch oven or large pot, heat 1 tablespoon of the olive oil over medium-high heat until it just starts to shimmer. Add the venison and cook, breaking it up with a spoon and stirring occasionally, for 10 minutes, or until cooked through. Using a slotted spoon, transfer the venison to a bowl. Drain the fat from the pot.

Return the pot to the stovetop, add the remaining 1 tablespoon olive oil, and heat over medium-high heat until it just starts to shimmer. Add the onions, garlic, bell peppers, and poblanos and cook for 8 minutes, stirring occasionally or until the onions are just translucent and the peppers have softened. Stir in the chili powder, ancho chile powder, cumin, onion powder, paprika, oregano, thyme, and salt and cook for 1 minute.

Return the meat to the pot. Add the beans, tomatoes, and wine and stir well. Bring the mixture to a boil, then reduce the heat to low, cover the pot with the lid ajar, and simmer, stirring occasionally, for 1 hour.

Stir in the vinegar and season the chili with salt. Serve topped with cheddar cheese and sour cream and garnished with scallions.

Calypso
TURKEY SLIDERS

※ *Makes 8 sliders* ※

⅓ cup garlic croutons, finely ground in a food processor

1 large egg

4 scallions, white parts only, thinly sliced (about ½ cup)

¼ cup chili sauce

2 garlic cloves, minced

2 teaspoons grated fresh ginger

½ teaspoon jerk seasoning powder (see Charlie's Tip)

⅓ cup dried cranberries

1 pound ground turkey

8 slider rolls

Pickles, for serving (optional)

Pickled red onions, for serving (optional)

Heat a grill to high.

In a large bowl, combine the ground croutons, egg, scallions, chili sauce, garlic, ginger, jerk seasoning, cranberries, and turkey. Using your hands, gently fold the mixture together until well combined.

Divide the mixture into 8 equal portions. Wet your hands and shape each portion into a small, 3½-inch patty.

Spray each burger with cooking spray and grill for 2 to 3 minutes per side.

Serve on slider rolls, with a pickle and pickled red onions, if desired.

CHARLIE'S TIP

Allspice and Scotch bonnet peppers (or other super-hot chiles) are essential ingredients in jerk seasoning, and they are usually combined with a mixture of garlic, thyme, nutmeg, and other spices. The blend originates from Jamaica and can be found as a paste or powdered dry rub. In this recipe, we use powdered jerk seasoning.

Calypso Turkey Sliders with Green Bean Fries (page 146)

Green Bean
FRIES

6 slices white bread

1 teaspoon sea salt

½ teaspoon onion powder

½ teaspoon garlic powder

4 cups chicken broth or
vegetable broth

10 ounces fresh green beans

4 to 8 cups vegetable or canola oil,
for frying

1 cup all-purpose flour

1 large egg

1 cup whole milk

Ranch dressing, for serving

Wasabi paste or powder, or your
favorite dipping sauce, for serving

Line a rimmed baking sheet with parchment paper.

In a food processor, pulse the bread slices until they turn into fine crumbs. Transfer the crumbs to a shallow bowl and add the salt, onion powder, and garlic powder. Stir to combine and set aside.

Fill a large bowl with ice and water and set it nearby. Pour the broth into a large microwave-safe bowl and add the green beans. Microwave on high for 5 minutes. Drain the beans and immediately submerge them in the ice water to cool.

Fill a large heavy pot or Dutch oven with oil to a depth of at least 1 to 2 inches. Heat the oil over medium-high heat until it registers 350°F on a deep-fry or candy thermometer (if you don't have a thermometer, see Charlie's Tip). Line a large plate with paper towels and set it nearby.

While the oil heats, place the flour in a pie pan or other shallow dish. In a second shallow dish, whisk together the egg and milk. Arrange the dishes with the flour, the egg-milk mixture, and the breadcrumbs on your work surface in assembly-line fashion.

Remove a handful of beans from the ice water and shake off the excess water. Dredge the beans in the flour, then the egg mixture, and finally in the breadcrumbs. Place them on the prepared baking sheet. Repeat to coat the remaining beans.

Working in batches to avoid crowding the pot, gently slide the beans into the hot oil and fry for 1 to 2 minutes, until golden brown. Use a slotted spoon or fry spider to transfer the beans to the paper towel–lined plate to drain.

Serve the green bean fries hot, with a side of ranch dressing combined with some wasabi paste or powder or your favorite dipping sauce.

CHARLIE'S TIP

If you're cooking for a crowd, you can easily double this recipe to serve eight, which you may want to do anyway, because these crispy "fries" disappear in the blink of an eye.

If you don't have a deep-fry or candy thermometer, dip the handle of a wooden spoon into the oil to test the temperature; if the oil bubbles, it's hot enough. You can also test the temperature by sliding one bean into the hot oil; if the oil is hot enough, the bean should sizzle and not sink. If it does sink, remove the bean, continue heating the oil for a minute or two more, and try again.

You never want your oil to start smoking. If this happens, immediately remove it from the heat (and remove any food that may be in the oil) and let the oil cool to 350°F before continuing to fry.

Chocolate Bourbon Pecan
BREAD PUDDING

⸙ Serves 12 ⸙

FOR THE CARAMEL SAUCE

1¼ cups sugar

¼ cup light corn syrup

1 tablespoon fresh lemon juice

1¼ cups heavy cream

1 cup pecans, toasted (see Charlie's Tip, page 34) and chopped

3 tablespoons bourbon

FOR THE PUDDING

Butter, for the pan

1 (1-pound) unsliced egg bread loaf, crusts trimmed, cut into 1-inch pieces (see Charlie's Tip, page 150)

2 cups whole milk

2 cups heavy cream

1 cup sugar

8 ounces dark chocolate (70% cacao), chopped

8 large eggs

1 tablespoon pure vanilla extract

Make the caramel sauce: In a heavy saucepan, combine the sugar and ½ cup water and heat over medium heat, stirring, until the sugar dissolves. Stir in the corn syrup and lemon juice and raise the heat to high. Without stirring, bring the mixture to a boil and cook, brushing down the sides of the pan with a wet pastry brush and swirling the pan occasionally, until the syrup turns a deep amber color. Remove the pan from the heat. Slowly pour in the cream (use caution, as the mixture will bubble up and sputter). Return the pan to the stovetop over low heat and stir until the caramel is melted and smooth. Raise the heat to high, bring the caramel to a boil, and cook, stirring often, until it has reduced to 1⅔ cups, about 4 minutes. Remove the pan from the heat. Stir in the pecans and the bourbon. (The caramel sauce can be made up to 2 days ahead. Cover and refrigerate until ready to use. Reheat in a small saucepan over low heat before using.)

Make the pudding: Grease a 9 x 13-inch glass baking dish with butter. Arrange the bread pieces evenly in the prepared baking dish. Set aside.

RECIPE CONTINUES

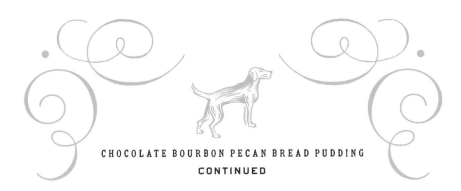

CHOCOLATE BOURBON PECAN BREAD PUDDING
CONTINUED

In a large heavy saucepan, combine the milk, cream, and sugar. Heat over medium-high heat, stirring, until the sugar has dissolved and the mixture comes to a boil. Remove from the heat. Add the chocolate and stir until the chocolate has melted and the mixture is well combined and smooth. Let the mixture cool so it's room temperature to the touch.

In a large bowl, whisk together the eggs and vanilla until well combined. Gradually whisk in the chocolate mixture. Pour the mixture over the bread pieces in the prepared baking dish, gently pressing down on the bread pieces using an offset spatula or the back of a spoon to make sure they're submerged. Let stand for 30 minutes.

Meanwhile, preheat the oven to 350°F.

Cover the baking dish with aluminum foil and bake until the pudding is set in the center, about 45 minutes. Remove from the oven, uncover, and let cool for at least 15 minutes before serving.

To serve, spoon the bread pudding into bowls or onto plates and ladle the warm caramel sauce over the top.

CHARLIE'S TIP

While egg breads, such as brioche or challah, are ideal for bread pudding, day old baguettes, country loaves, or sourdough loaves work well, too; they'll perhaps have more flavor but a slightly less creamy texture.

If you have any leftover caramel sauce, warm it and serve over vanilla ice cream.

Zink and Leader, two famous Radnor hounds

FULL CRY DINNER

Classic Whiskey Sour 154

Creamy Mushroom Tart 157

Belgian Beef Stew 158

Carrots au Gratin 160

Brussels Sprout Salad with Mustard Vinaigrette 162

Malted Milk Ball Cake 163

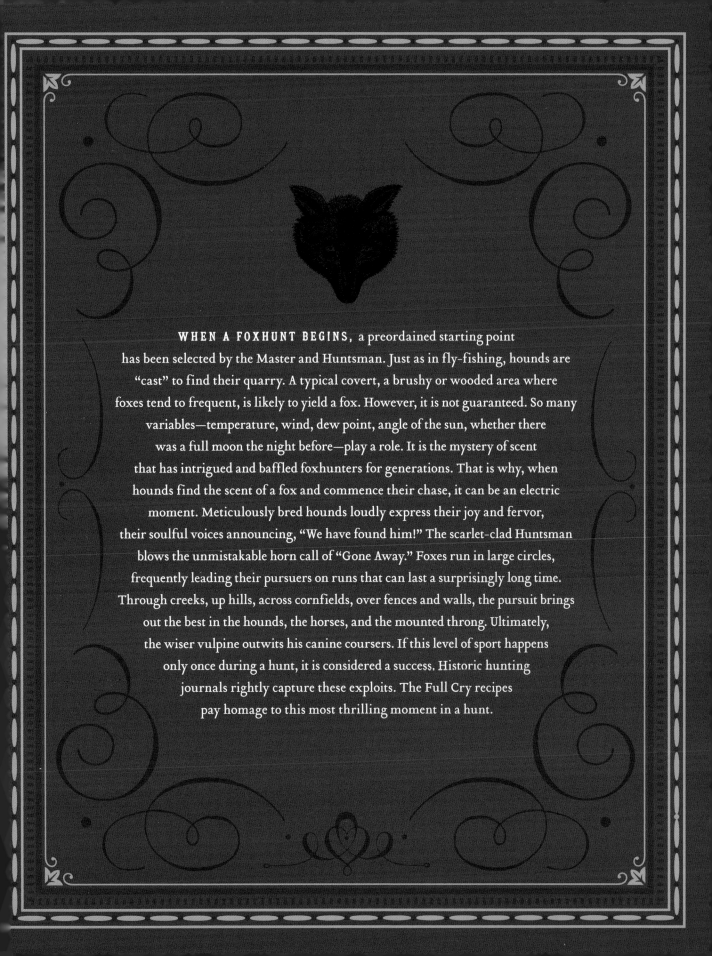

WHEN A FOXHUNT BEGINS, a preordained starting point
has been selected by the Master and Huntsman. Just as in fly-fishing, hounds are
"cast" to find their quarry. A typical covert, a brushy or wooded area where
foxes tend to frequent, is likely to yield a fox. However, it is not guaranteed. So many
variables—temperature, wind, dew point, angle of the sun, whether there
was a full moon the night before—play a role. It is the mystery of scent
that has intrigued and baffled foxhunters for generations. That is why, when
hounds find the scent of a fox and commence their chase, it can be an electric
moment. Meticulously bred hounds loudly express their joy and fervor,
their soulful voices announcing, "We have found him!" The scarlet-clad Huntsman
blows the unmistakable horn call of "Gone Away." Foxes run in large circles,
frequently leading their pursuers on runs that can last a surprisingly long time.
Through creeks, up hills, across cornfields, over fences and walls, the pursuit brings
out the best in the hounds, the horses, and the mounted throng. Ultimately,
the wiser vulpine outwits his canine coursers. If this level of sport happens
only once during a hunt, it is considered a success. Historic hunting
journals rightly capture these exploits. The Full Cry recipes
pay homage to this most thrilling moment in a hunt.

Classic

WHISKEY SOUR

⊰⊱ Makes 1 drink ⊰⊱

Handful of ice

1½ ounces whiskey

1 ounce fresh lemon juice

½ ounce Simple Syrup
(recipe follows)

2 ounces seltzer water

Maraschino cherry, for garnish

Orange slice, for garnish

In a highball glass filled with ice, add the whiskey, lemon juice, and Simple Syrup and stir. Top off with the seltzer and stir again. Garnish with the maraschino cherry and orange slice. Serve immediately.

SIMPLE SYRUP

Makes about 1½ cups

1 cup sugar

In a small saucepan, combine the sugar and 1 cup water and bring the mixture to a boil over high heat. Reduce the heat to medium and simmer until the sugar has dissolved, about 3 minutes.

Remove from the heat and let cool completely. Store in an airtight container in the refrigerator for up to 1 month.

Creamy
MUSHROOM TART

Serves 6

1 sheet frozen puff pastry, thawed

3 slices bacon, cut into small pieces

2 tablespoons finely chopped
    sweet onion

8 ounces cremini mushrooms,
    cleaned and sliced
    (about 1¼ cups)

1 garlic clove, minced

½ teaspoon sea salt

¼ teaspoon freshly ground black
    pepper

1 teaspoon Italian seasoning

2 tablespoons dry white wine or
    vegetable broth

½ (8-ounce) package cream cheese

¼ cup shredded Swiss cheese

Preheat the oven to 400°F.

Roll out the puff pastry to fit an 8-inch square tart pan with a removable bottom. Press the pastry into the pan. (Alternatively, if you don't have a tart pan, line a baking sheet with parchment paper and form the puff pastry into an 8-inch square on the prepared pan.) Refrigerate the pastry crust while you prepare the filling.

In a medium skillet, cook the bacon over medium-high heat, stirring occasionally, for about 2 minutes, until some of the fat has rendered. Add the onion and ¼ cup of the mushrooms, reduce the heat to medium, and cook until the mushrooms are softened and the onion is translucent, about 10 minutes. Stir in the garlic, salt, pepper, and Italian seasoning and cook for another minute. Add the wine and cook, scraping up the browned bits from the bottom of the pan and stirring them into the mixture, until the liquid has mostly evaporated, another minute or so. Add the cream cheese, reduce the heat to medium-low, and stir until melted and combined.

Remove the pan from the heat and stir in the Swiss cheese.

Remove the puff pastry crust from the refrigerator and spoon the filling evenly into the crust. Arrange the remaining mushrooms decoratively over the top. Bake for 15 minutes, or until the puff pastry is golden brown and the filling just begins to turn golden. Remove from the oven, cut into squares, and serve.

Belgian
BEEF STEW

Serves 6 to 8

4 slices thick-cut bacon, cut into 1-inch pieces

½ cup all-purpose flour

½ teaspoon sea salt, plus more to taste

¼ teaspoon freshly ground black pepper, plus more to taste

3 pounds boneless beef chuck, cut into 1½-inch cubes

4 tablespoons extra-virgin olive oil

2½ pounds sweet onions, thinly sliced

12 ounces Trappist ale or other full-bodied Belgian ale

1 cup beef broth

1 tablespoon packed brown sugar

1 tablespoon red wine vinegar

1 dried bay leaf

¼ teaspoon dried thyme, crumbled

In a Dutch oven or large pot, cook the bacon over medium heat, stirring occasionally, until golden, about 8 minutes. Using tongs, transfer the bacon to a large plate lined with paper towels and set aside, leaving the rendered fat in the pot.

In a shallow bowl, stir together the flour, salt, and pepper. Dredge the meat cubes in the flour mixture and set aside.

Add 1 tablespoon of the olive oil to the rendered bacon fat in the pot and heat over medium heat until hot but not smoking. Working in batches to avoid crowding the pan, add the beef and cook until browned on all sides. Add 1 to 2 tablespoons more oil, if needed. Transfer the browned beef to the plate with the bacon.

Preheat the oven to 325°F. Position a rack in the lower third of the oven.

Add the remaining 1 tablespoon olive oil to the pot and heat over medium heat. Add the onions and cook, stirring occasionally, until soft and golden brown, 15 to 20 minutes. If the onions begin to stick, add a few tablespoons water at a time, up to ½ cup. Add the ale and broth and bring to a boil, scraping up any browned bits from the bottom of the pot and stirring them into the mixture. Stir in the brown sugar, vinegar, bay leaf, and thyme and season with salt and pepper.

Return the beef and bacon to the pot and bring the mixture to a boil. Cover and transfer the pot to the oven. Braise until the beef is tender, 2 hours to 2 hours 30 minutes.

Remove from the oven and discard the bay leaf before serving. The stew may be made up to 3 days in advance.

· FOXHUNTING ·
ETIQUETTE

- *Never get between staff and hounds, unless requested by staff. And do not rate (reprimand) a hound; that is the job of the staff.*

- *Turn your horse's head toward passing staff and hounds when standing. This allows your horse to see the hounds approach and not be surprised. Never permit your horse to kick a hound; horses that have any habit of kicking out at hounds should not be in the hunt field.*

- *If your horse kicks at other horses, it is only considerate to braid a red ribbon in its tail and ride at the rear of the field if possible.*

CARROTS
au Gratin

↣ *Serves 6* ↢

12 carrots (about 2½ pounds), peeled and sliced into 2-inch matchsticks

4 tablespoons (½ stick) unsalted butter

1 tablespoon all-purpose flour

2 cups whole milk

3 cups shredded sharp cheddar cheese

½ teaspoon sea salt

⅛ teaspoon ground white pepper

½ cup breadcrumbs

Preheat the oven to 350°F.

Bring a large pot of water to a boil over high heat. Add the carrots. When the water returns to a boil, cook the carrots for 3 minutes. Drain the carrots and set aside.

In a large skillet, melt the butter over medium-high heat. Sprinkle in the flour and stir well to combine. Slowly whisk the milk into the flour mixture. While whisking continuously, bring the mixture to a slow simmer, 5 to 7 minutes. The sauce will start to thicken. When it is the consistency of heavy cream and can coat the back of a spoon, stir in the cheese, sea salt, and the white pepper. Reduce the heat to low and stir until the cheese has melted and the sauce is creamy.

Arrange the carrots evenly in a 2-quart baking dish and pour the cheese sauce over the carrots. Lightly dust the top with the breadcrumbs. Bake for 30 to 45 minutes, until the top is bubbling and browned. Serve immediately.

Brussels Sprout
SALAD
WITH MUSTARD VINAIGRETTE

⋙ *Serves 6* ⋘

⅔ cup walnut halves

1 pound Brussels sprouts, very
    thinly sliced (see Charlie's Tip)

⅔ cup dried cherries

3 tablespoons fresh lemon juice

1 tablespoon sherry vinegar

½ teaspoon sea salt

1 tablespoon Dijon mustard

½ cup extra-virgin olive oil

3 tablespoons walnut oil

4 ounces goat cheese, crumbled

Freshly ground black pepper

Preheat the oven to 350°F.

Place the walnuts on a rimmed baking sheet and toast in the oven for 5 to 10 minutes, until they start to become golden and fragrant. Set aside to cool.

In a large serving bowl, combine the Brussels sprouts and cherries.

In a small bowl, combine the lemon juice, vinegar, and salt. Whisk in the mustard, then, while whisking, stream in the olive oil and walnut oil and whisk until emulsified.

Chop the toasted nuts and sprinkle them over the Brussels sprouts. Pour the dressing over the salad and toss to combine. Sprinkle with the goat cheese and season with pepper. Serve at room temperature.

CHARLIE'S TIP

If you are short on time, look for pre-shaved Brussels sprouts, available in many grocery store produce sections. You can also vary the cheese-nut-fruit combination to your liking—try blue cheese, pecans, and cranberries. The salad can be made up to 2 hours in advance and kept in the refrigerator. Bring to room temperature before serving.

Malted Milk Ball
CAKE

⚜ Makes one 9-inch cake ⚜

FOR THE CAKE

Nonstick baking spray

1 cup whole milk

1 cup malted milk powder

2¼ cups cake flour

1¼ cups granulated sugar

¾ cup cocoa powder

1½ teaspoons baking soda

1 teaspoon baking powder

½ teaspoon sea salt

1 cup vegetable oil

3 large eggs

1 cup sour cream

1½ teaspoons pure vanilla extract

FOR THE FROSTING

18 ounces semisweet chocolate chips

4½ tablespoons dark cocoa powder

3 cups (6 sticks) unsalted butter, at
    room temperature

6 tablespoons whole milk

2¼ teaspoons pure vanilla extract

4½ cups sifted confectioners' sugar

½ cup chopped pistachios (optional)

Large malted milk balls for
    decorating the cake

Make the cake: Preheat the oven to 350°F. Spray three 9-inch round cake pans with baking spray and line the bottoms of the pans with parchment paper cut to fit.

In a small bowl, stir together the milk and malted milk powder until the milk powder has dissolved. Set aside.

In a large bowl, whisk together the flour, granulated sugar, cocoa powder, baking soda, baking powder, and salt. Add the milk mixture, vegetable oil, and eggs and beat with a wooden spoon (or handheld mixer) until smooth. Stir in the sour cream and vanilla until just combined.

Divide the batter among the prepared pans. Bake for 20 to 25 minutes, until a wooden toothpick or skewer inserted into the center of each cake comes out clean. Transfer the pans to a wire rack to cool for 15 minutes. Turn the cakes out onto the rack and let cool completely.

RECIPE CONTINUES

MALTED MILK BALL CAKE
CONTINUED

Make the frosting: In a small saucepan, melt the chocolate over low heat, then remove the pan from the heat. Whisk in the cocoa powder, 1 tablespoon at a time, until completely smooth. Set aside to cool slightly.

In a large bowl using a handheld mixer, beat the butter on medium speed for 3 minutes, or until creamy. Slowly add the milk and beat until smooth. Add the melted chocolate and vanilla, and beat well for 5 minutes more. Add the confectioners' sugar, ½ cup at a time, beating on low speed between each addition until the frosting is creamy and easily spreadable. You may need to add either a little more milk or a little more confectioners' sugar to get the right consistency.

Trim the tops of the cakes to level them, if desired, then set one cake layer upside down on a serving plate. Frost the top of the cake and sprinkle with chopped pistachios, if desired, then set a second cake layer on top and frost that as well, again adding pistachios if you'd like. Set the final cake layer upside down on top and frost the top and sides of the cake. Decorate the top of the cake with the malted milk balls, starting in the center and working your way outward. Slice and serve. Store, covered, at room temperature for up to 4 days.

BITCHES' BRUNCH

Spicy Bloody Mary 168

Homemade Dill Pickles 171

Irish Oatmeal Brûlée with Ginger Cream 172

Poached Eggs on Brioche with Spinach, Spicy Bacon
& Béarnaise Sauce 175

Hash Browns & Roasted Peppers 178

Sicilian Rice Salad 179

Creole Shrimp 180

Sour Cream Coffee Cake 183

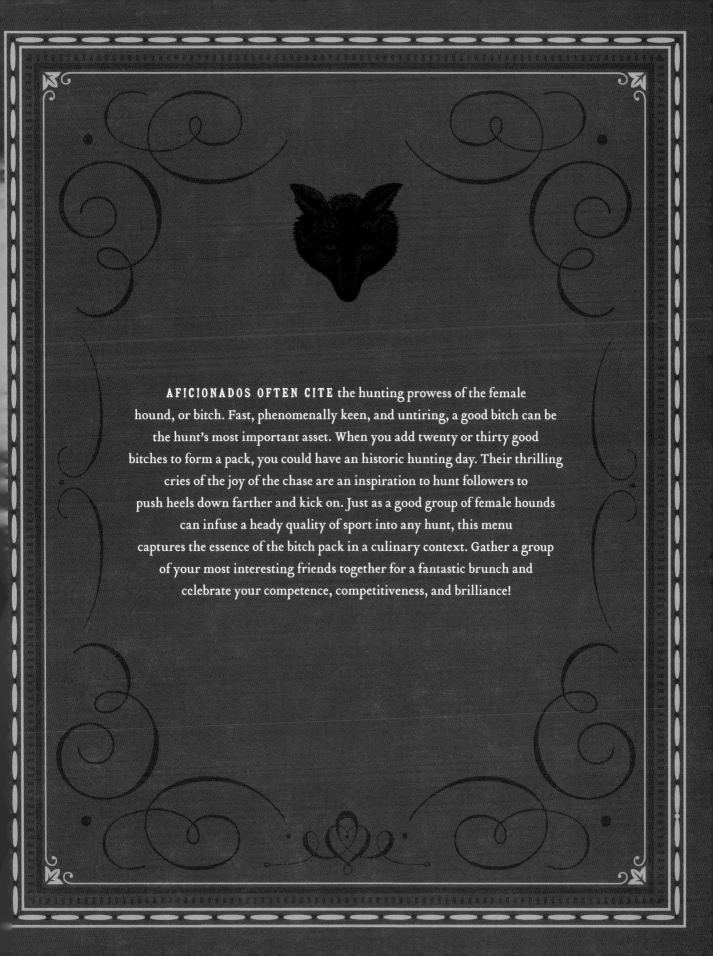

AFICIONADOS OFTEN CITE the hunting prowess of the female hound, or bitch. Fast, phenomenally keen, and untiring, a good bitch can be the hunt's most important asset. When you add twenty or thirty good bitches to form a pack, you could have an historic hunting day. Their thrilling cries of the joy of the chase are an inspiration to hunt followers to push heels down farther and kick on. Just as a good group of female hounds can infuse a heady quality of sport into any hunt, this menu captures the essence of the bitch pack in a culinary context. Gather a group of your most interesting friends together for a fantastic brunch and celebrate your competence, competitiveness, and brilliance!

Spicy
BLOODY MARY

⁘⁘ Make 6 drinks ⁘⁘

48 ounces tomato juice

5 tablespoons prepared horseradish

3 tablespoons Worcestershire sauce

1 tablespoon celery salt

1 tablespoon garlic powder

½ teaspoon freshly ground black pepper

20 to 30 dashes of Tabasco sauce

Lemon or lime slices (optional)

1 tablespoon smoked paprika (optional; see Charlie's Tip)

1 tablespoon kosher salt (see Charlie's Tip)

About 3 cups ice

12 ounces vodka

Any combination of the following garnishes (see Charlie's Tip): celery stalks, pimento-stuffed olives, peperoncini, pickled okra, meat sticks such as Slim Jims, bacon, shrimp, or cubes of cheese

In a large pitcher, combine the tomato juice, horseradish, Worcestershire, celery salt, garlic powder, pepper, and Tabasco. Refrigerate until ready to serve, ideally overnight.

When you're ready to assemble the drinks, salt the rims of the glasses, if desired: On a small plate, mix the paprika and kosher salt. Rub the rim of an 8-ounce glass with a lemon or lime slice, then dip the rim into the paprika mixture and twist to coat. Repeat to rim all the glasses.

Fill the rimmed glasses with ice. Add 2 ounces of vodka to each glass, then top with the tomato mixture. Garnish as desired and serve.

CHARLIE'S TIP

There are many types of seasonings you can use for rimming the Bloody Mary glasses. Instead of smoked paprika and kosher salt, try 1 tablespoon celery salt and 1 tablespoon kosher salt, or even just 2 tablespoons Old Bay seasoning.

For a festive presentation, combine several garnishes on a short decorative skewer and rest it across the top of the glass.

*Spicy Bloody Mary with Homemade
Dill Pickles (page 171)*

Homemade
DILL PICKLES

※ *Makes 32 pickles* ※

7½ cups distilled white vinegar

4 heads garlic, cloves separated, smashed, and peeled

1 tablespoon mustard seeds

1 tablespoon whole black peppercorns

2 teaspoons allspice berries

1 teaspoon celery seed

1 teaspoon coriander seed

½ cup sea salt

16 Kirby cucumbers (about 3 pounds), ends trimmed, halved lengthwise

2 bunches fresh dill

In a medium pot, combine the vinegar, garlic, mustard seeds, peppercorns, allspice, celery seed, coriander, salt, and 2½ cups water. Bring the mixture to a boil over high heat and simmer for 1 minute.

Divide the cucumbers and dill evenly between two ½-gallon mason jars. Pour the vinegar-spice mixture over the cucumbers. Add more water if needed to completely submerge the pickles in brine. Cover tightly and refrigerate for up to 3 weeks. (You can eat them as soon as a few days, but they get better with age!)

· FOXHUNTING ·
ETIQUETTE

- *Alert those behind you to hazards: Call "Ware Hole" and point to it, also ware low branch, wire, glass, hound, car, etc. ("ware" is an abbreviation of beware).*

Irish Oatmeal
BRÛLÉE
WITH GINGER CREAM

Serves 8

FOR THE OATMEAL

8 cups whole milk

2 cups steel-cut oats

1 cinnamon stick

1 (3-inch) strip orange zest (peeled with a vegetable peeler)

Pinch of sea salt

¾ cup dried cranberries

½ cup golden raisins

½ cup pure maple syrup

½ cup packed brown sugar

FOR THE GINGER CREAM

1 cup heavy cream

2 (1-inch-thick) slices fresh ginger

1 cinnamon stick

2 tablespoons grated orange zest

6 tablespoons pure maple syrup

¼ teaspoon freshly grated nutmeg

Make the oatmeal: In a large heavy saucepan, bring the milk to a low simmer over medium heat. Add the oats, cinnamon stick, orange zest, and salt. Reduce the heat to the lowest setting and simmer, stirring occasionally, for 30 minutes, until the mixture is thick and creamy. Remove the pan from the heat and discard the cinnamon stick and orange peel. Stir in the cranberries, raisins, and maple syrup.

Preheat the broiler to high. Position a rack 5 inches below the heating element. Divide the oats among eight ungreased 6-ounce ramekins. Place the ramekins on a baking sheet and sprinkle the brown sugar evenly among the ramekins. Broil for 4 to 7 minutes, or until the sugar is caramelized. Be sure to keep an eye on these while they broil as they quickly go from browned to burned.

Meanwhile, make the ginger cream: In a small saucepan, combine the cream, ginger, cinnamon stick, and orange zest. Bring the mixture barely to a simmer over medium heat, reduce the heat to low, and gently simmer for 10 minutes. Remove the pan from the heat. Using a slotted spoon, remove and discard the ginger and cinnamon stick. Stir in the maple syrup and nutmeg. Serve the oatmeal brûlée with the warm ginger cream.

Poached Eggs on Brioche with Spinach, Spicy Bacon & Béarnaise Sauce with Hash Browns & Roasted Peppers (page 178)

POACHED EGGS

on Brioche

WITH SPINACH, SPICY BACON & BÉARNAISE SAUCE

⁂ Serves 6 ⁂

½ cup brown sugar

1 teaspoon cayenne pepper

1½ teaspoons black pepper

1 pound thick-cut bacon, cut into
    3-inch pieces

1 tablespoon unsalted butter

1 shallot, minced

12 ounces baby spinach

3 tablespoons distilled white vinegar

6 thick slices brioche

6 large eggs

1 cup Béarnaise Sauce (recipe follows)

Preheat the oven to 350°F. Line two large rimmed baking sheets with aluminum foil and place an oven-safe wire rack on top of each pan.

In a large bowl, stir together the brown sugar, cayenne, and black pepper. Dip the bacon into the sugar mixture, thoroughly coating each piece. Transfer the coated bacon to the wire racks. Bake for 30 to 35 minutes, until crispy. Watch carefully so the bacon doesn't burn. Transfer the bacon to paper towels and let cool to room temperature.

Meanwhile, in a medium skillet, melt the butter over medium heat. Stir in the shallot and cook until translucent, about 5 minutes. Add the spinach and cook until wilted, about 3 minutes. Remove from the heat and set aside.

Fill a large pot with water, add the vinegar, and bring the mixture to a boil over high heat.

Meanwhile, toast the bread slices until golden brown. Place each one on its own serving plate. Dividing the bacon evenly, lay 4 or so strips on each slice of toast. Top with 2 tablespoons of the spinach mixture.

Once the water boils, reduce the heat to maintain a simmer. Crack an egg into a small bowl and slowly pour it into the simmering water. Repeat with the remaining eggs. Cook until the whites are cooked through and firm but the yolks are still soft, about 3 minutes. Use a slotted spoon to remove the eggs, one at a time, and place one directly on top of each bread-bacon-spinach combo. Top with Béarnaise Sauce and serve.

RECIPE CONTINUES

BÉARNAISE SAUCE

Makes 1 cup

½ cup fresh tarragon, minced

1 large shallot, minced

¼ cup tarragon vinegar

¼ cup white wine

4 egg yolks, clean of all egg whites

2 tablespoons fresh lemon juice

1 cup (2 sticks) unsalted butter,
melted and kept very hot

In a small saucepan, combine the tarragon, shallot, vinegar, and wine and bring the mixture to a simmer over medium heat. Reduce the heat to low and cook the mixture until there is no more liquid. Set aside to cool completely.

Meanwhile, in a food processor, combine the egg yolks and lemon juice. With the motor running, slowly add the hot melted butter through the feed tube. The mixture should thicken and become smooth and creamy (see Charlie's Tip, if your sauce breaks or appears clumpy). Add the shallot-tarragon mixture and process for 10 seconds, or until combined. If needed, refrigerate the sauce to thicken. Store in an airtight container in the refrigerator for up to 3 days.

CHARLIE'S TIP

*Béarnaise sauce (also Hollandaise Sauce, page 222) can be tricky.
Sometimes the sauce "breaks," which happens when the butter and eggs don't emulsify, and
instead of a smooth, luxurious sauce, you end up with a grainy mixture. Because of this,
we like to make it right before guests arrive, just in case it doesn't come together.
If this happens, transfer the broken sauce to a bowl, clean out the food processor bowl, and put
1 tablespoon fresh lemon juice and 1 tablespoon of the broken sauce back into the
food processor bowl. Process until the mixture emulsifies, then continue adding the broken
sauce, a tablespoon or two at a time, until the mixture comes together. To be safe,
you can make the sauce up to several days in advance and reheat it very slowly in a
double boiler just before serving.*

HASH BROWNS
& ROASTED PEPPERS

⟿ Serves 6 ⟾

3 tablespoons unsalted butter, plus more as needed

3 tablespoons extra-virgin olive oil, plus more as needed

1 large red onion, diced

¼ cup roasted red peppers, diced (see Texas Caviar Dip, page 68, for how to roast peppers)

4 large white potatoes, peeled and cut into 1-inch pieces

Sea salt and freshly ground black pepper

In a large skillet, heat 1 tablespoon each of the butter and olive oil over medium-high heat until the butter has melted. Add the onion and roasted peppers and cook, stirring occasionally, for 8 to 10 minutes, until the peppers are softened and the onion is golden brown. Transfer the mixture to a serving bowl. Set aside.

Add the remaining 2 tablespoons each of butter and olive oil to the skillet and heat over medium until the butter has melted. Add the potatoes and cook, stirring occasionally, for 20 minutes, until browned. Add more oil and/or butter to the pan as needed to keep the potatoes from sticking. Return the onion-pepper mixture to the skillet and toss to combine. Cook until the mixture is heated through. Season generously with salt and black pepper.

Transfer the potatoes to the serving bowl. Serve immediately.

Sicilian
RICE SALAD

≫≫ Serves 8 ≪≪

FOR THE SALAD

6 cups cooked rice

1 pound large cooked shrimp, peeled and cut in half

¾ cup chopped red onions

2 (15-ounce) cans quartered artichoke hearts, drained

¼ cup drained capers

⅓ cup chopped fresh dill

2 cups chopped mixed red, yellow, and orange bell peppers

FOR THE DRESSING

¾ cup vegetable oil

¼ cup red wine vinegar

1 or 2 garlic cloves, minced

¼ teaspoon dried basil

¼ teaspoon dried oregano

Sea salt and freshly ground black pepper

⅓ cup chopped flat-leaf parsley, for garnish

Make the salad: In a large bowl, toss together all the ingredients for the salad.

Make the dressing: In a jar with a lid, combine all the ingredients for the dressing, cover, and shake well to combine. Pour the dressing over the salad and toss to coat evenly. Refrigerate for several hours before serving.

Garnish with parsley and serve at room temperature.

Creole
SHRIMP

❦ Serves 6 as an appetizer or side dish ❦

24 jumbo shrimp, peeled (tails left on) and deveined

½ teaspoon sea salt

1 teaspoon Creole seasoning

Freshly ground black pepper

3 garlic cloves, minced

1 tablespoon chopped fresh rosemary

⅓ cup fresh lemon juice

¼ cup Worcestershire sauce

1½ teaspoons hot sauce

½ cup (1 stick) unsalted butter

Put the shrimp in a large bowl and sprinkle with the salt, Creole seasoning, and pepper to taste. Add the garlic, rosemary, lemon juice, Worcestershire, and hot sauce and toss to combine.

In a large skillet, melt the butter over medium heat. Add the shrimp and cook, stirring, for 3 to 4 minutes, just until they turn pink. Do not overcook the shrimp.

Remove the shrimp from the pan and serve immediately.

· FOXHUNTING ·
ETIQUETTE

- *Close the gate if you are the last one through it.*

- *Replace rails you knock down. If a rail is broken, be sure to tell one of the Masters so that the hunt can attend to its replacement.*

Sour Cream
COFFEE CAKE

≈ Makes one 10-inch Bundt cake ≈

1 cup (2 sticks) unsalted butter, plus
    more for the pan

1 cup chopped walnuts

¼ cup packed brown sugar

1 teaspoon ground cinnamon

2 cups all-purpose flour

1 teaspoon baking powder

¼ teaspoon sea salt

2 cups granulated sugar

2 large eggs

1 cup sour cream

1 teaspoon pure vanilla extract

Preheat the oven to 350°F. Generously butter a 10-inch Bundt pan.

In a small bowl, combine the walnuts, brown sugar, and cinnamon and set aside.

In a separate small bowl, whisk together the flour, baking powder, and salt and set aside.

In the bowl of a stand mixer fitted with the paddle attachment, cream the butter and granulated sugar on medium speed until light and fluffy, about 5 minutes. Add the eggs one at a time, beating well after each addition. Add the sour cream and vanilla and beat on low until just combined. Add the dry ingredients and mix on low until blended.

Spoon half the batter into the prepared pan. Sprinkle half the walnut mixture over the batter. Do not let the walnut mixture touch the sides of the pan. Top with the remaining batter and sprinkle with the remaining walnut mixture.

Bake for 45 minutes to 1 hour, until a wooden toothpick or skewer inserted into the center of the cake comes out clean. Remove from the oven and let cool in the pan on a wire rack for 15 minutes.

Turn the cake out onto a serving plate and let cool completely before slicing and serving.

MASTERS' MENU

Earl Grey Gin & Tonic 186

Chutney Cheese Pâté 187

Grilled Pork Tenderloin with Apricot
& Horseradish Sauce 188

Spring Pea Risotto 190

Roasted Brussels Sprouts with Bacon & Sriracha Aïoli 191

Russian Tea Cakes 196

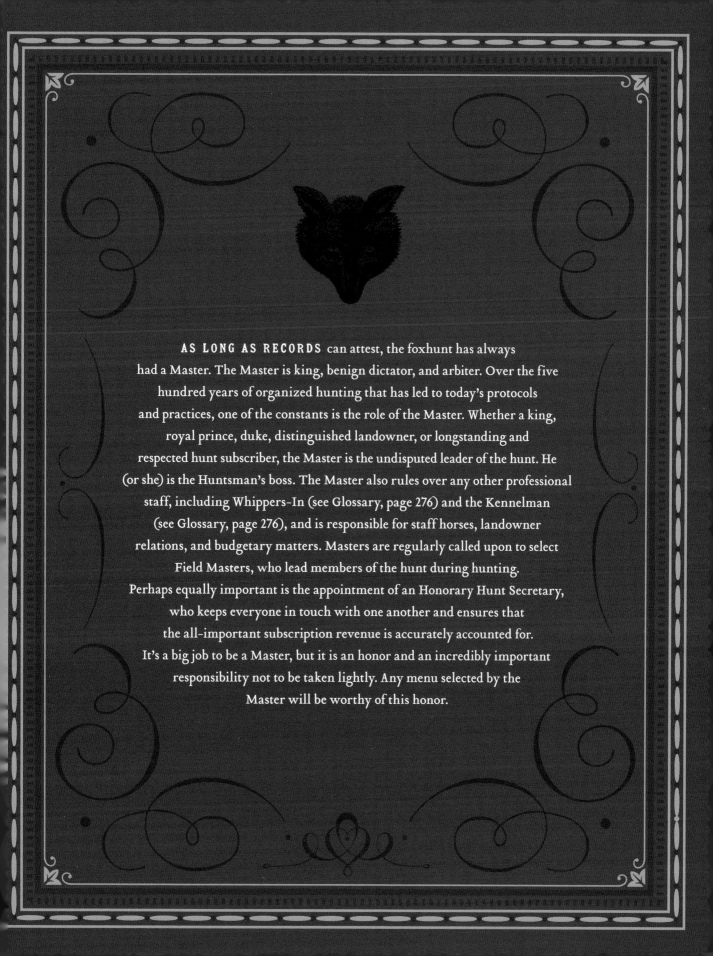

AS LONG AS RECORDS can attest, the foxhunt has always
had a Master. The Master is king, benign dictator, and arbiter. Over the five
hundred years of organized hunting that has led to today's protocols
and practices, one of the constants is the role of the Master. Whether a king,
royal prince, duke, distinguished landowner, or longstanding and
respected hunt subscriber, the Master is the undisputed leader of the hunt. He
(or she) is the Huntsman's boss. The Master also rules over any other professional
staff, including Whippers-In (see Glossary, page 276) and the Kennelman
(see Glossary, page 276), and is responsible for staff horses, landowner
relations, and budgetary matters. Masters are regularly called upon to select
Field Masters, who lead members of the hunt during hunting.
Perhaps equally important is the appointment of an Honorary Hunt Secretary,
who keeps everyone in touch with one another and ensures that
the all-important subscription revenue is accurately accounted for.
It's a big job to be a Master, but it is an honor and an incredibly important
responsibility not to be taken lightly. Any menu selected by the
Master will be worthy of this honor.

Earl Grey
GIN & TONIC

※ *Makes 1 drink* ※

Handful of ice

2 ounces Earl Grey–Infused Gin
(recipe follows)

3 ounces tonic water, such as Fever-
Tree or Q Tonic, plus more to taste

Lemon slice, for garnish

Fill a highball glass with ice. Pour in the Earl Grey-Infused Gin and top with the tonic water. Stir and garnish with the lemon slice. Serve immediately.

EARL GREY–INFUSED GIN

Makes about 12 drinks

1 (750 ml) bottle neutral gin, such as
Beefeater

3 tablespoons loose Earl Grey tea

Place the gin and tea leaves in a large mason jar or lidded container, stir well to combine, and cover. Allow the leaves to infuse the gin for 3 to 4 hours. Strain the gin through a fine-mesh strainer into a pitcher. Using a funnel, pour the tea-infused gin back into the original gin bottle. Store as you would non-infused gin.

CHARLIE'S TIP

You may substitute decaffeinated Earl Grey tea here, or try any number of herbal teas, such as lemon or blackberry.

Chutney CHEESE PÂTÉ

1 (8-ounce) package cream cheese, at room temperature

½ cup grated sharp cheddar cheese

2 teaspoons dry sherry

½ teaspoon curry powder

¼ teaspoon sea salt, plus more to taste

¼ cup chopped mango chutney

3 scallions, white parts only, chopped

Crackers, for serving

In a large bowl using a handheld mixer, beat the cream cheese on medium speed until light and fluffy. Add the cheddar cheese, sherry, curry powder, and salt and beat again until combined. Spread the mixture over the bottom of a 6-inch serving dish, cover with plastic wrap, and refrigerate until ready to serve.

Spread the chutney evenly over the cheese mixture and sprinkle with the scallions. Serve with crackers.

Grilled
PORK TENDERLOIN
WITH APRICOT & HORSERADISH SAUCE

⚜ Serves 6 to 8 ⚜

¾ cup apricot preserves

¾ cup prepared horseradish

2 tablespoons extra-virgin olive oil

4 garlic cloves, minced

¼ teaspoon sea salt

¼ teaspoon freshly ground black pepper

2 pounds pork tenderloin (about 2 tenderloins), trimmed of visible fat

Heat an outdoor grill to high or a grill pan over high heat.

In a high-speed blender or food processor, puree the apricot preserves and horseradish until smooth. Transfer the mixture to a bowl and set aside.

In a small bowl, combine the olive oil, garlic, salt, and pepper. Place the tenderloins on a platter and rub generously with the mixture; let sit for a few minutes. Reserve any remaining marinade.

Grill the tenderloins for 15 to 20 minutes, turning frequently and brushing with the reserved marinade. The pork is done when a meat thermometer inserted into the center registers 150 to 155°F or the inside is barely pink. Transfer the meat to a cutting board and let stand for 5 minutes before carving.

To serve, slice the tenderloins and place on a serving plate. Drizzle with the apricot-horseradish sauce, or serve it on the side.

CHARLIE'S TIP

The combination of apricot and horseradish makes for a zesty sauce that is a perfect accompaniment to most any meat—or anything breaded and fried!

*Grilled Pork Tenderloin with
Apricot & Horseradish Sauce and
Spring Pea Risotto (page 190)*

Spring Pea
RISOTTO

❈ Serves 6 ❈

6 cups chicken broth

4 tablespoons (½ stick) unsalted
butter

2 tablespoons extra-virgin olive oil

1 large shallot, minced

1 garlic clove, minced

1½ cups Arborio rice

½ cup dry white wine

1½ cups frozen peas, thawed

¾ cup grated Parmesan cheese, plus
more for serving

1 tablespoon fresh lemon juice

¼ teaspoon freshly grated nutmeg

1½ teaspoons kosher salt

Freshly ground black pepper

¼ cup fresh mint, chopped, plus a
few small mint leaves for garnish

In a medium saucepan, bring the broth to a slow simmer over medium heat, then cover and reduce the heat to the lowest setting to keep the broth warm.

In a large skillet, heat 2 tablespoons of the butter and the olive oil over medium-high heat until the butter has melted. Add the shallots and garlic and cook, stirring continuously, until softened, about 8 minutes.

Add the rice and stir to coat with the butter-shallot mixture. Pour in the wine and simmer until the liquid has evaporated. Reduce the heat to medium and add just enough of the warm broth to cover the rice, about 1 cup. Cook, stirring continuously, until the liquid has been absorbed; adjust the heat as needed to keep the liquid at a low simmer. Repeat, adding 1 cup of the broth at a time and cooking until it has been absorbed and the rice is creamy and slightly al dente, 20 to 25 minutes (you may not need all the broth).

Stir in the peas and cook until heated through, about 2 minutes. Stir in the remaining 2 tablespoons butter, the cheese, lemon juice, and nutmeg. Add a splash more broth if necessary to loosen the risotto. Season with salt and pepper and stir in the mint.

Transfer the risotto to a serving bowl and garnish with the mint leaves. Serve with additional cheese on the side.

Roasted
BRUSSELS SPROUTS

WITH BACON & SRIRACHA AÏOLI

※ Serves 6 ※

FOR THE BRUSSELS SPROUTS

Nonstick cooking spray

12 ounces thick-cut bacon

¾ cup diced red onion

4 pounds Brussels sprouts, trimmed and halved

¼ cup honey

3 tablespoons apple cider vinegar

⅓ cup dried sweetened cranberries

¼ teaspoon sea salt

¼ teaspoon freshly ground black pepper

FOR THE SRIRACHA AÏOLI

½ cup mayonnaise

2 tablespoons sriracha

1½ tablespoons fresh lemon juice

Sea salt

Make the Brussels sprouts: Preheat the oven to 400°F. Spray a rimmed baking sheet with cooking spray.

In a large skillet, cook the bacon over medium-high heat until just crispy. Transfer the bacon to a paper towel–lined plate. Discard all but ¼ cup of the rendered fat in the skillet.

Add the red onion to the rendered fat in the skillet and cook over medium heat, stirring continuously to prevent burning, for 6 to 8 minutes, until tender. Add the Brussels sprouts and toss to combine. Pour the contents of the skillet onto the prepared baking sheet and bake for 20 minutes.

RECIPE CONTINUES

ROASTED BRUSSELS SPROUTS WITH
BACON & SRIRACHA AÏOLI
CONTINUED

Meanwhile, in a small bowl, stir together the honey and vinegar.

Remove the Brussels sprouts from the oven, stir in the dried cranberries, and sprinkle with the honey mixture. Return the baking sheet to the oven and bake for 5 minutes more, or until the Brussels sprouts are browned and tender. Remove from the oven. Chop the bacon and sprinkle over the Brussels sprouts. Season with the salt and pepper.

Make the sriracha aïoli: In a small bowl, whisk together the mayonnaise, sriracha, and lemon juice and season with salt.

Place the warm Brussels sprouts on a serving platter and drizzle with the aïoli. Serve immediately.

- *If the field is asked by the Field Master to reverse, do so as quickly as possible. You are usually being asked to reverse to clear the way for the staff and hounds while they are running.*

Russian
TEA CAKES

⋙ *Makes 2½ dozen cookies* ⋘

1 cup (2 sticks) unsalted butter, at
room temperature

1 cup confectioners' sugar

1 teaspoon pure vanilla extract

2¼ cups all-purpose flour

½ cup chopped pecans

In a large bowl using a handheld mixer, cream the butter, ½ cup of the confectioners' sugar, and the vanilla on medium-high speed until light and fluffy, about 5 minutes. Slowly add the flour and beat on medium until fully combined. Add the nuts and mix to combine. Refrigerate the dough, covered, for 1 hour.

Preheat the oven to 400°F. Line two rimmed baking sheets with parchment paper.

Shape the chilled dough into 1-inch balls and place them 1 inch apart on the prepared baking sheets. Bake for 9 minutes (see Charlie's Tip), then remove from the oven and let cool on the baking sheets set on wire racks.

Place the remaining ½ cup confectioners' sugar in a small bowl. When the cookies are cool enough to handle, roll them in the confectioners' sugar to coat. Serve. Store in an airtight container at room temperature for up to 5 days.

CHARLIE'S TIP

There are no indicators as to when the cookies are done—they do not brown or change appearance—so just take them out of the oven after the indicated cooking time. Be sure not to overbake them. When baked correctly, the cooled cookie should melt in your mouth. These cookies also freeze very well.

SPRING FLING

Devon Julep 200

Moroccan Lamb Lettuce Cups 202

Hearty Skillet Chicken 205

Roasted Sweet Potatoes & Bacon 206

Asparagus with Hazelnuts & Tarragon Vinaigrette 209

Poppy Seed Almond Cake with Balsamic Berries 210

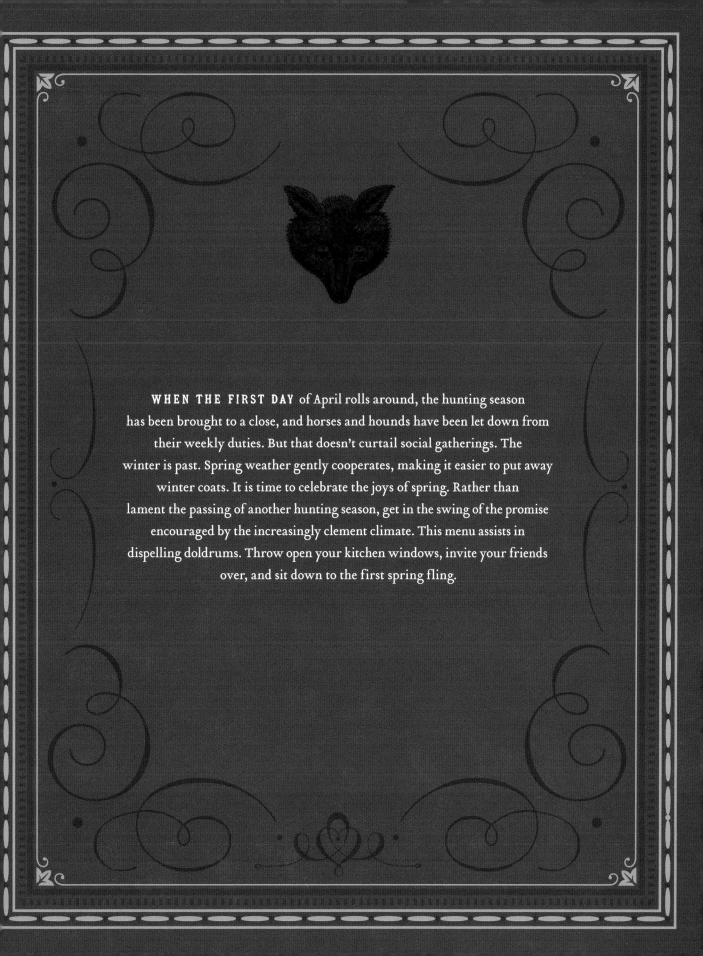

WHEN THE FIRST DAY of April rolls around, the hunting season
has been brought to a close, and horses and hounds have been let down from
their weekly duties. But that doesn't curtail social gatherings. The
winter is past. Spring weather gently cooperates, making it easier to put away
winter coats. It is time to celebrate the joys of spring. Rather than
lament the passing of another hunting season, get in the swing of the promise
encouraged by the increasingly clement climate. This menu assists in
dispelling doldrums. Throw open your kitchen windows, invite your friends
over, and sit down to the first spring fling.

DEVON JULEP

Makes 1 drink

6 fresh mint leaves

1½ ounces bourbon

Handful of ice

½ ounce vodka

½ ounce white crème de menthe

1 ounce seltzer water

Tear up 4 of the mint leaves and place them in the bottom of a lowball or old-fashioned glass. Pour in the bourbon and muddle the mint and bourbon together using a muddler or spoon. Fill the glass with ice. Add the vodka and crème de menthe and stir. Top off the drink with the seltzer and stir. Garnish with the remaining mint leaves and serve.

· FOXHUNTING ·
ETIQUETTE

- *Ride around seeded, planted fields—never over them. In general, avoid lawns, driveways, and houses but always follow the instructions of the Field Master, as certain landowners have specific preferences as to how we pass through their property.*

- *Always acknowledge landowners or farmers and thank them.*

Devon Julep with Moroccan Lamb Lettuce Cups (page 202)

Moroccan Lamb
LETTUCE CUPS

Serves 8

FOR THE LAMB

1 tablespoon extra-virgin olive oil

1 pound ground lamb

2 garlic cloves, minced

Juice of 1 large lemon (about 3 tablespoons)

1 tablespoon Moroccan spice blend, such as ras el hanout (see Charlie's Tip)

½ teaspoon sea salt

Freshly ground black pepper

1 tablespoon tomato paste

½ cup chopped fresh mint

3 scallions, white parts only, minced

FOR THE SAUCE

⅔ cup plain Greek yogurt

1 garlic clove, minced

1 teaspoon tahini

1 teaspoon sriracha, or other hot sauce

FOR SERVING

8 large green-leaf or Boston lettuce leaves

2 scallions, minced

¼ cup chopped fresh mint

Make the lamb: In a large skillet, heat the olive oil over medium-high heat until it just starts to shimmer. Add the lamb and cook, stirring occasionally and breaking it up with a wooden spoon, until cooked through, about 10 minutes. Stir in the garlic, lemon juice, spice blend, salt, and pepper to taste and cook for 1 minute. Add the tomato paste, mint, and scallions and stir to combine. Reduce the heat to medium and cook for 2 to 3 minutes so the flavors can meld, then remove from the heat.

Make the sauce: In a small bowl, stir together the yogurt, garlic, tahini, and sriracha.

To serve, arrange the lettuce leaves on a platter and spread with the sauce. Top evenly with the lamb, scallions, and mint. Serve immediately.

CHARLIE'S
TIP

Ras el hanout *is Arabic for "head of the shop," a reference to the spices
in the blend being the best the spice seller has to offer. Hailing from North Africa, it's typically
made from a mixture of coriander, cumin, red pepper flakes, cinnamon, paprika,
cardamom, ginger, and turmeric, but the spices may vary depending on the region or the person
preparing the blend. Ras el hanout can be purchased online at thespicehouse.com
or in many gourmet grocery stores.*

Held every year at Radnor Hunt, the Bryn Mawr Hound Show is one of the oldest in the country.

Hearty
SKILLET CHICKEN

3 tablespoons extra-virgin olive oil

1 (4-pound) whole chicken

Salt and freshly ground black pepper

1 fennel bulb, sliced lengthwise into ½-inch-thick pieces

2 large carrots, peeled and sliced into ½-inch-thick rounds

1 bunch scallions, white parts only, cleaned and left whole

3 wide strips lemon zest (peeled with a vegetable peeler)

1 lemon, cut into wedges, for serving

Preheat the oven to 425°F.

In a large ovenproof skillet, heat 1 tablespoon of the olive oil over medium-high heat. Season the chicken inside and out with salt and pepper and add to the skillet, breast-side down. Cook, using tongs to rotate the chicken and being careful not to tear the skin, until browned on all sides, 12 to 15 minutes. Transfer the chicken to a plate.

In the same skillet, heat the remaining 2 tablespoons olive oil over medium-high heat. Stir in the fennel, carrots, scallions, and lemon zest, season with salt and pepper, and toss to combine.

Place the chicken breast-side up on top of the vegetables, transfer the skillet to the oven, and roast for 35 to 40 minutes, until a meat thermometer inserted into the thickest part of the thigh (without touching the bone) registers 165°F. Transfer the chicken to a cutting board and let rest for at least 10 minutes before carving.

Transfer the roasted vegetables to a platter. Carve the chicken and arrange it on the platter over or next to the vegetables. Spoon the pan juices over the chicken and vegetables. Serve with lemon wedges.

Roasted
SWEET POTATOES
& BACON

⟶ Serves 4 to 6 ⟵

2 pounds sweet potatoes, scrubbed and cut into 1-inch cubes

2 tablespoons extra-virgin olive oil

½ teaspoon sea salt, plus more to taste

½ teaspoon red pepper flakes

6 ounces pancetta or bacon, chopped

1 tablespoon unsalted butter

1 large red onion, thinly sliced

3 tablespoons pure maple syrup

3 tablespoons red wine vinegar

Freshly ground black pepper

Preheat the oven to 425°F. Put the sweet potatoes on a rimmed baking sheet, sprinkle with the olive oil, salt, and red pepper flakes, and toss to combine. Roast, stirring occasionally, until the potatoes are fork-tender and they just begin to brown, about 45 minutes.

While the potatoes are cooking, put the bacon in a large skillet and cook over medium heat, stirring occasionally, until crisp, 5 to 8 minutes. Using a slotted spoon, remove the bacon from the pan and set aside.

Add the butter and onion to the skillet and reduce the heat to medium-low. Cook the onion, stirring occasionally until soft and browned, about 10 minutes. Stir in the maple syrup and vinegar and cook until the liquid has thickened some and reduced to a few tablespoons. Transfer the reserved bacon and sweet potatoes to the skillet and stir to combine. Season with salt and black pepper to taste. Serve warm.

ASPARAGUS

WITH HAZELNUTS & TARRAGON VINAIGRETTE

Serves 6

1 pound asparagus, trimmed

2 small shallots, chopped

3 tablespoons white wine vinegar

1 tablespoon chopped fresh tarragon, or 1¼ teaspoons dried

1 teaspoon Dijon mustard

5 tablespoons extra-virgin olive oil

Sea salt and freshly ground black pepper

¼ cup hazelnuts, toasted, skinned, and coarsely chopped (see Charlie's Tip)

Fill a pot with an inch or two of water and set a steamer basket inside. Bring the water to a boil over high heat. Fill a large bowl with ice and water and set it nearby. Add the asparagus to the steamer basket, cover, and steam until the asparagus is fork-tender, 4 to 6 minutes. Do not overcook the asparagus. Using tongs, immediately transfer the asparagus to the ice water and let cool for 1 minute. Drain the asparagus and transfer it to a paper towel–lined plate to dry.

In a small bowl, combine the shallots, vinegar, tarragon, and mustard. While whisking, gradually stream in the olive oil and whisk until emulsified. Season with salt and pepper.

Arrange the asparagus on a platter. Drizzle with the vinaigrette and sprinkle with the hazelnuts. Serve.

CHARLIE'S TIP

To toast and skin hazelnuts, preheat the oven to 375°F. Spread the nuts in a single layer on a rimmed baking sheet and toast in the oven for about 10 minutes. Remove from the oven and let cool for several minutes. Lay a dish towel out on the counter and spread the hazelnuts out on it. Lay another dish towel on top and rub the nuts between the two towels to remove the skins.

The vinaigrette can be made up to a day in advance, and the asparagus can be prepared 6 hours in advance, covered, and refrigerated.

Poppy Seed
ALMOND CAKE
WITH BALSAMIC BERRIES

Makes one 9 x 5-inch loaf

FOR THE CAKE

Butter, for the pan

1½ cups cake flour (see Charlie's
   Tip, page 213), plus more for
   the pan

¾ teaspoon baking powder

¼ teaspoon sea salt

2½ ounces almond paste, cut into
   small pieces (optional)

1¼ cups granulated sugar

⅓ cup canola or vegetable oil

2 large eggs, at room temperature

2 tablespoons poppy seeds

¾ teaspoon pure almond extract

½ cup whole milk

⅓ cup sliced almonds

FOR THE TOPPING

2 pints blueberries

2 pints strawberries

2 pints raspberries

½ bunch fresh mint, chopped

2 tablespoons balsamic vinegar

1 tablespoon honey

Confectioners' sugar, for dusting

Make the cake: Preheat the oven to 350°F. Grease a 9 x 5-inch loaf pan with butter and dust it with flour, tapping out any excess.

In a medium bowl, sift together the flour, baking powder, and salt. Add the almond paste (if using) and stir.

In a large bowl, whisk together the granulated sugar, oil, eggs, poppy seeds, and almond extract until blended. Whisk in the flour mixture in three additions, alternating with the milk, beginning and ending with the flour mixture.

RECIPE CONTINUES

POPPY SEED ALMOND CAKE
WITH BALSAMIC BERRIES
CONTINUED

Pour the batter into the prepared pan. Sprinkle the almonds evenly over the top. Bake for 1 hour to 1 hour 15 minutes, until the top is deep brown and a wooden toothpick or skewer inserted into the center comes out clean. Remove from the oven and let cool in the pan on a wire rack for 10 minutes. Invert the cake onto the rack, turn it right-side up, and let cool completely.

Make the topping: In a medium bowl, combine the berries, mint, vinegar, and honey and toss gently to combine. Let stand for 1 hour.

Dust the cake with confectioners' sugar and cut into ½-inch slices. Top each slice with a spoonful of the berries and serve.

CHARLIE'S TIP

You can substitute 1 cup minus 2 tablespoons all-purpose flour for 1 cup of the cake flour.

This cake makes a great gift because it keeps well, and it also freezes well. To freeze, wrap the loaf in a layer of plastic wrap, then a layer of aluminum foil, and place it in a plastic zip-top bag and seal. Allow the cake to come to room temperature before serving.

TALLYHO, LET'S EAT!

Pomegranate-Rosemary Gin Cocktail 217

Grilled Peaches with Serrano Ham 218

Veal Marsala with Gnocchi 219

Roasted Cauliflower with Hollandaise Sauce 222

Gluten-Free Walnut Rosemary Coconut Cake 225

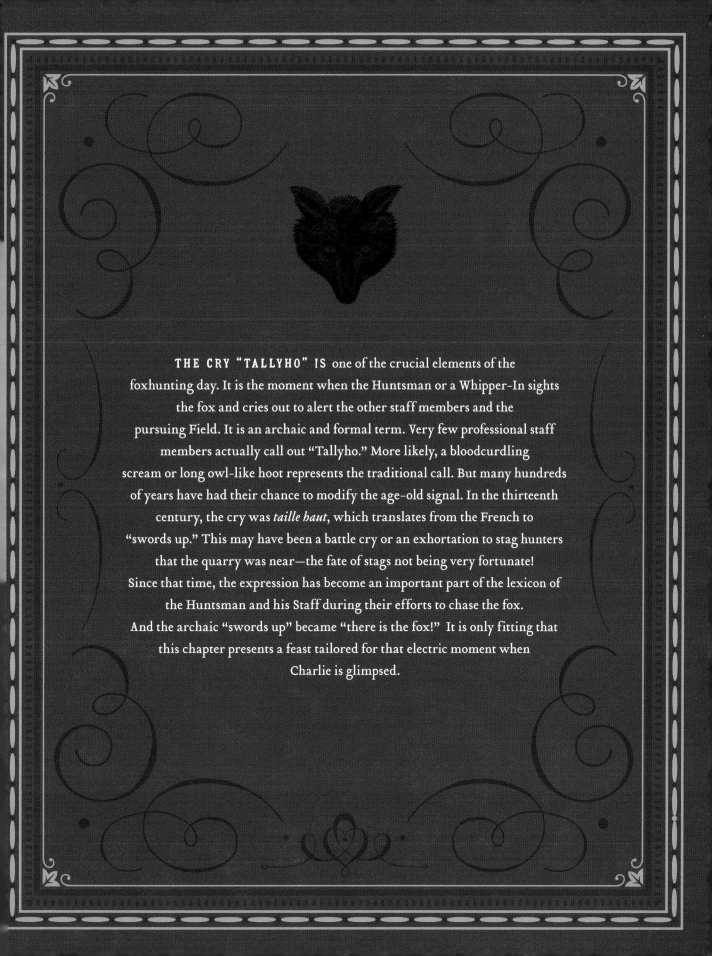

THE CRY "TALLYHO" IS one of the crucial elements of the
foxhunting day. It is the moment when the Huntsman or a Whipper-In sights
the fox and cries out to alert the other staff members and the
pursuing Field. It is an archaic and formal term. Very few professional staff
members actually call out "Tallyho." More likely, a bloodcurdling
scream or long owl-like hoot represents the traditional call. But many hundreds
of years have had their chance to modify the age-old signal. In the thirteenth
century, the cry was *taille haut*, which translates from the French to
"swords up." This may have been a battle cry or an exhortation to stag hunters
that the quarry was near—the fate of stags not being very fortunate!
Since that time, the expression has become an important part of the lexicon of
the Huntsman and his Staff during their efforts to chase the fox.
And the archaic "swords up" became "there is the fox!" It is only fitting that
this chapter presents a feast tailored for that electric moment when
Charlie is glimpsed.

*Pomegranate–Rosemary
Gin Cocktail with Grilled
Peaches with Serrano
Ham (page 218)*

Pomegranate-Rosemary
GIN COCKTAIL

Makes 1 drink

Handful of ice

2 ounces Hendrick's gin or other high-quality gin

1½ ounces pomegranate juice

2 ounces Rosemary–Brown Sugar Syrup (recipe follows)

3 ounces seltzer water

1 small sprig fresh rosemary

10 pomegranate seeds

Fill a highball glass with ice. Pour in the gin, pomegranate juice, and Rosemary–Brown Sugar Syrup. Top with the seltzer. Garnish with the rosemary sprig and pomegranate seeds. Serve immediately.

ROSEMARY–BROWN SUGAR SYRUP

Makes about 1½ cups

1 cup packed light brown sugar

6 sprigs fresh rosemary

In a small saucepan, combine 1 cup water, the brown sugar, and the rosemary. Heat over medium heat, stirring, until the sugar dissolves, then simmer for 1 minute. Remove the pan from the heat and let cool for 2 hours.

Strain the syrup through a fine-mesh strainer and discard the solids. Store in an airtight container in the refrigerator for up to 2 months.

FOXHUNTING ETIQUETTE

- *If you view a fox out of sight of any of the staff, wait for the fox to be far enough away that you won't alarm it, then call "Tallyho" and point your hat.*

GRILLED PEACHES

WITH SERRANO HAM

⚒ Makes 24 pieces, to serve 6 ⚒

3 peaches, halved and pitted

2 to 3 teaspoons extra-virgin olive oil

¼ teaspoon ground cumin

12 thin slices serrano ham (about 4 ounces)

24 fresh basil leaves

3 tablespoons balsamic glaze (see Charlie's Tip)

Heat a grill to medium.

In a medium bowl, toss the peaches with the oil and cumin and let stand for 10 minutes.

Grill the peaches for 4 to 5 minutes on each side. Transfer to a cutting board and let cool, then cut each half into quarters to yield 24 slices total.

Cut each slice of ham in half lengthwise. (It may be easier to roll up each slice first, cut it in half, then unroll it.)

Place a slice of peach about 1 inch from the top of a piece of ham. Top the peach with a basil leaf and roll the peach in the ham. Set the roll on a platter and repeat with the remaining peaches, ham, and basil.

Drizzle with the balsamic glaze and serve.

CHARLIE'S TIP

Balsamic glaze is one of our favorite pantry staples. It's a terrific addition to salads and meat sauces, and it can even be drizzled on berries for dessert. You can find it bottled in most grocery stores, with higher quality types available at specialty markets. To make your own balsamic glaze, in a small saucepan, boil ¾ cup balsamic vinegar over high heat for 6 minutes, or until reduced to 3 tablespoons. Set aside to cool and use as desired.

The ham-wrapped peach slices can be assembled up to 2 hours in advance and refrigerated. Bring them to room temperature and drizzle with the balsamic glaze just before serving.

VEAL MARSALA

WITH GNOCCHI

Serves 4

4 teaspoons sea salt, plus more for seasoning

1 (8-ounce) package fresh gnocchi

4 veal cutlets (about 4 ounces each)

¼ cup all-purpose flour

4 tablespoons extra-virgin olive oil

2 cups sliced white mushrooms

2 garlic cloves, minced

1 cup chicken broth

1 cup sweet Marsala wine

½ cup dry white wine

2 tablespoons dry red wine

Juice of 1 lemon (about 3 tablespoons)

Pinch of ground coriander

Pinch of cayenne pepper

Pinch of dried oregano

Pinch of dried rosemary

Freshly ground black pepper to taste

Preheat the oven to 200°F.

Fill a large pot with water and add 1 tablespoon of the salt. Bring the water to a boil. Add the gnocchi and cook according to the package directions. Drain and set aside.

Place the veal between two pieces of plastic wrap or parchment or waxed paper and pound using a meat mallet or rolling pin until very thin, about ⅛ inch thick (see Charlie's Tip, page 221).

In a shallow bowl, stir together the flour and remaining 1 teaspoon salt. Dredge the cutlets in the flour until completely coated and set aside.

In a large skillet, heat 2 tablespoons of the olive oil over high heat until it starts to shimmer. Sear the cutlets, in batches if necessary, until golden brown, about 1½ minutes per side. Transfer the cutlets to an oven-safe plate, cover with aluminum foil, and place in the oven to keep warm.

In the same skillet, heat 1 tablespoon of the olive oil over medium-high heat until it starts to shimmer. Add the mushrooms and cook, stirring, until softened, about 7 minutes. Transfer the mushrooms to a plate.

RECIPE CONTINUES

Add the remaining 1 tablespoon oil to the skillet and heat until it starts to shimmer. Add the garlic and cook, stirring, for 30 seconds. Add the broth, Marsala, white and red wines, lemon juice, coriander, cayenne, oregano, and rosemary. Bring the mixture to a boil, stirring and scraping any browned bits from the bottom of the pan to combine them with the sauce, then reduce the heat to low. Simmer, stirring occasionally, for 20 minutes, or until reduced by half. Season with salt and black pepper to taste. Return the mushrooms and any juices that have accumulated on the plate to the sauce as well as the gnocchi. Using a large spoon, gently turn the gnocchi and the mushrooms in the sauce to combine.

Serve the veal with the mushrooms and gnocchi ladled over the top.

CHARLIE'S TIP

Pounding the cutlets may seem like an unnecessary step, but it helps tenderize the meat, breaking down the connective muscle tissues and flattening the meat to a uniform thickness so it cooks evenly and quickly. Overcooking veal can cause it to become too tough. If you don't have a meat mallet or rolling pin, you can also use the bottom of a heavy skillet (cast iron works great!), a wine bottle, or even a cookbook (sure, go ahead and use this one!).

Roasted CAULIFLOWER
WITH HOLLANDAISE SAUCE

⁓ Serves 4 to 6 ⁓

1 whole cauliflower

2 tablespoons extra-virgin olive oil

Flaky sea salt, such as Maldon

1 cup Hollandaise Sauce (recipe follows)

Preheat the oven to 375°F.

Carefully cut the core from the cauliflower, leaving the cauliflower head intact. Generously cover the entire cauliflower with olive oil and season with flaky salt.

Place the cauliflower cored-side down in a cast-iron skillet and cover the entire skillet with foil. Bake for 30 minutes. Uncover and use a metal spatula to loosen the cauliflower from the skillet. Bake, uncovered, for 1 hour more, or until browned. Remove from the oven. Slice into wedges and serve topped with Hollandaise Sauce, or alongside as preferred.

HOLLANDAISE SAUCE

⁓ Makes 1 cup ⁓

4 egg yolks, clean of all egg whites

2 tablespoons fresh lemon juice

1 cup (2 sticks) unsalted butter, melted and kept very hot

In a food processor, combine the egg yolks and lemon juice and process for 20 seconds, or until combined. With the motor running, slowly add the hot melted butter through the feed tube. The mixture should thicken and become smooth and creamy (if your sauce breaks or appears clumpy, see Charlie's Tip on page 176). Store in an airtight container in the refrigerator for up to 3 days.

Gluten-Free Walnut Rosemary
COCONUT CAKE

⁓ Makes one 8-inch cake ⁓

FOR THE CAKE

Gluten-free nonstick baking spray

1 cup gluten-free all-purpose flour (see Charlie's Tip, page 226)

½ cup gluten-free ancient grains flour (see Charlie's Tip, page 226)

¼ teaspoon baking soda

¼ teaspoon baking powder

¼ teaspoon sea salt

1 tablespoon finely chopped fresh rosemary

½ cup buttermilk

1 teaspoon pure rosemary extract (see Charlie's Tip, page 226)

1 cup granulated sugar

½ cup canola oil

2 large eggs

½ cup chopped walnuts

½ cup sweetened flaked coconut

FOR THE SYRUP

6 tablespoons granulated sugar

1 tablespoon unsalted butter

1 teaspoon pure rosemary extract (see Charlie's Tip, page 226)

Confectioners' sugar, for dusting

Make the cake: Preheat the oven to 350°F. Spray an 8-inch springform pan with baking spray and line the bottom with parchment paper cut to fit. Wrap the outside of the pan with two layers of aluminum foil.

In a medium bowl, combine both flours, the baking soda, baking powder, salt, and fresh rosemary.

In a small bowl, stir together the buttermilk and rosemary extract.

In the bowl of a stand mixer fitted with the paddle attachment, beat the granulated sugar, oil, and eggs on high speed for 2 minutes. Add the flour mixture in three additions, alternating with the buttermilk mixture, beginning and ending with the flour mixture. Beat well after each addition. Stir in the walnuts and coconut.

RECIPE CONTINUES

GLUTEN-FREE WALNUT ROSEMARY COCONUT CAKE
CONTINUED

Pour the mixture into the prepared pan. Bake for 1 hour to 1 hour 10 minutes, until a wooden toothpick or skewer inserted into the center comes out clean.

Meanwhile, make the syrup: In a small saucepan, combine the granulated sugar, butter, and 3 tablespoons water. Bring the mixture to a gentle boil over high heat, reduce the heat to low, and simmer for 5 minutes. Remove the syrup from the heat and stir in the rosemary extract.

Remove the cake from the oven, set the pan on a wire rack, and immediately pour the hot syrup over the cake. Let the cake cool in the pan for 4 hours. Release the sides of the springform pan and remove the ring. Invert the cake onto a plate, remove the bottom of the pan, peel off the parchment paper, and set the cake right-side up on a serving platter.

Dust with confectioners' sugar just before serving.

CHARLIE'S TIP

We find the combination of Cup4Cup Gluten-Free Flour and King Arthur Ancient Grains Flour Blend (made from 30 percent each amaranth, millet, and sorghum flours and 10 percent quinoa flour) works very well in this recipe. If gluten is not a concern for you, feel free to substitute equal amounts of all-purpose flour for the gluten-free flour. We still recommend using the Ancient Grains Flour Blend, though, as it provides nice flavor and texture.

You can find Star Kay White brand pure rosemary extract online and in some specialty gourmet stores.

Kirkwood Preserve, Willistown Conservation Trust

RADNOR FETE

Cucumber-Ginger Margarita 230

Fried Zucchini Ribbons with Tzatziki 236

Prosciutto, Arugula & Provolone Rolls 238

Easy Summer Pasta 241

Watermelon, Arugula & Feta Salad 242

Coconut Cheesecake 244

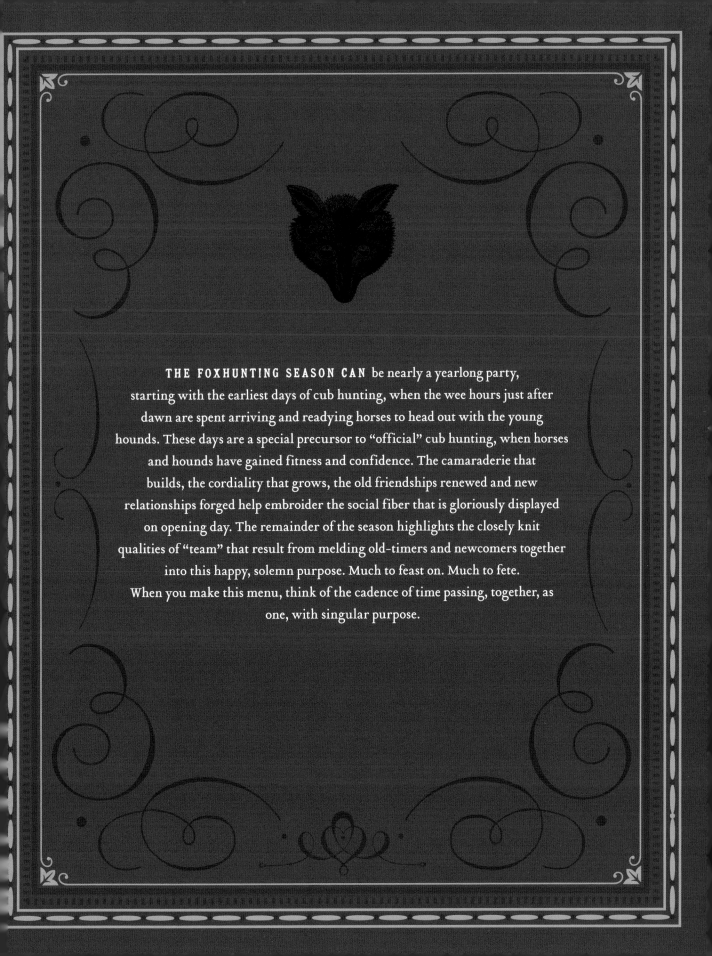

THE FOXHUNTING SEASON CAN be nearly a yearlong party, starting with the earliest days of cub hunting, when the wee hours just after dawn are spent arriving and readying horses to head out with the young hounds. These days are a special precursor to "official" cub hunting, when horses and hounds have gained fitness and confidence. The camaraderie that builds, the cordiality that grows, the old friendships renewed and new relationships forged help embroider the social fiber that is gloriously displayed on opening day. The remainder of the season highlights the closely knit qualities of "team" that result from melding old-timers and newcomers together into this happy, solemn purpose. Much to feast on. Much to fete. When you make this menu, think of the cadence of time passing, together, as one, with singular purpose.

Cucumber-Ginger
MARGARITA

⚜ Makes 1 drink ⚜

Kosher salt

Lime slice

Handful of ice

2 ounces reposado tequila

1 ounce Ginger-Lime Syrup (recipe follows)

1 ounce Cucumber Water (recipe follows)

1 ounce fresh lime juice

Pour a layer of salt onto a small plate. Wet the rim of a 16-ounce mason jar with the lime slice. Dip the rim in the salt to coat.

Fill the jar with ice. Add the tequila, Ginger-Lime Syrup, Cucumber Water, and lime juice and stir. Garnish with the lime slice and serve immediately.

RECIPE CONTINUES

· FOXHUNTING ·
ETIQUETTE

- *Do not crowd against other horses, do not let your horse forge ahead of others, forcing them off the path.*

*Cucumber-Ginger Margarita
with Fried Zucchini Ribbons with
Tzatziki (page 236)*

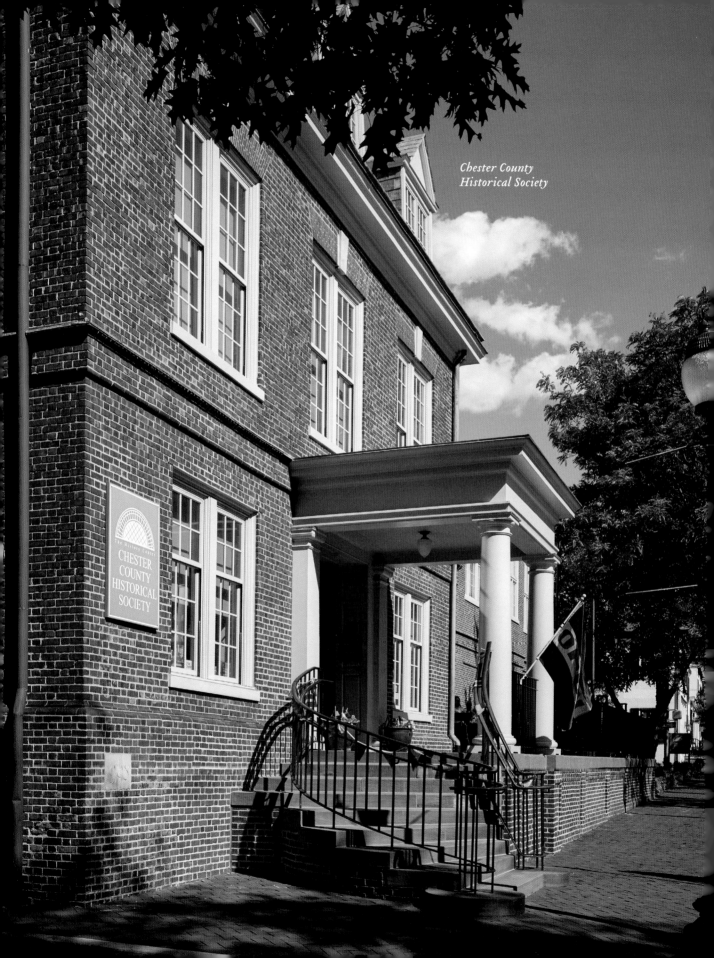

Chester County Historical Society

GINGER–LIME SYRUP

Makes about 1 cup

1 cup coarsely chopped peeled fresh
  ginger

1 cup sugar

Zest of 2 limes

In a food processor, combine the ginger, sugar, and lime zest and pulse until well combined (the mixture will be liquidy). Transfer the mixture to a small saucepan and add 1⅓ cups water. Bring to a boil over medium-high heat, then reduce the heat to medium-low and simmer for 5 minutes, or until the sugar dissolves, stirring occasionally. Remove the pan from the heat and let steep for 15 minutes. Strain the syrup through a fine-mesh sieve. Store in an airtight container in the refrigerator for up to 1 month.

CUCUMBER WATER

Makes 1 cup

1 cup chopped peeled cucumber

In a blender, combine the cucumber and 1 cup water. Puree until smooth. Use immediately or store in an airtight container in the refrigerator for up to 3 days.

Painting of "Radnor Hunt 125th Anniversary Meet" by artist Booth Malone

Fried
ZUCCHINI RIBBONS
WITH TZATZIKI

Serves 4

FOR THE TZATZIKI

½ English (seedless) cucumber, peeled and finely diced

2 cups plain Greek yogurt

4 garlic cloves, minced

⅓ cup chopped fresh dill

Juice of ½ lemon (about 1½ tablespoons)

Sea salt and freshly ground black pepper

FOR THE ZUCCHINI RIBBONS

4 to 8 cups canola oil, for frying

6 medium zucchini

1 large egg

1 cup buttermilk

¾ cup panko breadcrumbs

¾ cup seasoned breadcrumbs

½ cup grated Pecorino Romano cheese

Sea salt

Make the tzatziki: Wrap the cucumber in a piece of cheesecloth. Holding it over the sink, squeeze out any excess moisture. (Alternatively, put the cucumber in a fine-mesh strainer in the sink and press on it with the back of a spoon to extract excess moisture.)

Transfer the cucumber to a medium bowl, add the yogurt, garlic, dill, and lemon juice, and stir to combine. Season with salt and pepper. Cover and refrigerate the tzatziki for 2 hours so the flavors can blend (you can always serve it immediately, but it gets better the longer it sits).

Make the zucchini ribbons: Line two rimmed baking sheets with parchment paper.

Fill a large heavy pot or Dutch oven with oil to a depth of 1 to 2 inches. Heat the oil over medium-high heat until it registers 350°F on a deep-fry or candy thermometer (if you don't have a thermometer, see Charlie's Tip on page 147 for instructions on testing the oil temperature). Line a serving platter with paper towels and set it nearby.

While the oil heats, cut the ends off the zucchini and use a vegetable peeler to slice them into long strips. In a medium bowl, whisk together the egg and buttermilk. In a shallow bowl or pie plate, stir together the panko, seasoned breadcrumbs, and cheese. Dip the zucchini ribbons in the egg mixture, then in the breadcrumbs (you can do this a few ribbons at a time, just be sure they are thoroughly coated), and place them on the prepared baking sheets.

Working in batches to avoid crowding the pot, gently slide the zucchini ribbons into the oil and fry for 3 minutes, or until golden brown. Using a slotted spoon or fry spider, transfer the cooked zucchini strips to the paper towel–lined serving platter to drain. Sprinkle with salt.

Serve with the tzatziki sauce.

CHARLIE'S TIP

Because zucchini has such mild flavor, you can pair these ribbons with most any dipping sauce of your choice, such as ranch or blue cheese, in place of the tzatziki.

Prosciutto, Arugula & Provolone ROLLS

⧽⧽⧽ *Serves 8* ⧽⧽⧽

16 slices prosciutto (about 8 ounces)

1 (8-ounce) block sharp provolone cheese, cut into thirty-two 2-inch-long pieces

96 arugula leaves (about 2½ ounces)

3 tablespoons balsamic glaze, plus more to taste (see Charlie's Tip, page 218)

Cut each slice of prosciutto in half lengthwise. (It may be easier to roll up each slice first, cut it in half, then unroll it.) Place a piece of cheese about 1 inch from the top of a piece of prosciutto. Top with 3 arugula leaves and drizzle with a few drops of the balsamic glaze. Wrap the prosciutto around the cheese and arugula to form a roll. The prosciutto sticks to itself fairly well, so no need to secure the rolls with toothpicks. Place the roll on a serving platter and repeat with the remaining ingredients. Refrigerate, covered, until ready to serve.

Remove from the refrigerator 15 to 30 minutes prior to serving.

· FOXHUNTING · ETIQUETTE

• *Stop and be quiet at a check. Make sure that your horse can stand still when asked. Noise will distract the hounds, prevent staff from hearing what is happening, and possibly turn the fox, thereby potentially ruining the hunt.*

Easy SUMMER PASTA

Serves 6 to 8

6 large ripe tomatoes (about 2 pounds), seeded and chopped

4 teaspoons sea salt, plus more to taste

¼ cup extra-virgin olive oil

1½ cups packed fresh basil leaves (about 3 ounces), cut into thin ribbons (see Charlie's Tip)

9 garlic cloves, minced (about 3 tablespoons)

1½ pounds dry spaghetti

2 cups coarsely grated Locatelli or Pecorino Romano cheese (about 8 ounces), plus more for serving

Freshly ground black pepper

Place the tomatoes in a large wooden bowl and sprinkle with 1 teaspoon of the salt. Pour over ¼ cup of the olive oil and gently toss to combine. Cover and let stand for 2 hours, stirring occasionally.

Add the basil, garlic, and remaining ½ cup oil to the tomatoes and let stand for 1 hour more, stirring occasionally.

Meanwhile, fill a large pot with water and add the remaining 3 teaspoons salt. Bring the water to a boil. Add the pasta and cook according to the package directions until al dente (or 1 minute less than the standard time). Drain well.

Add the pasta to the bowl with the tomatoes and fold in the cheese. Use tongs to combine. Season with salt and pepper. Serve immediately, with extra cheese on the side.

CHARLIE'S TIP

Basil is a tender herb that bruises easily and often turns black when chopped. To preserve the basil's beautiful green color, cut the leaves into thin strips: Stack the leaves, roll the stack like a cigar, and thinly slice across the roll to create thin ribbons (this technique is called chiffonade).

Watermelon, Arugula & Feta SALAD

※ *Serves 6* ※

1 (5-ounce) package baby arugula

6 cups cubed seedless watermelon

1 pint yellow grape tomatoes, halved

7 ounces feta cheese, crumbled

½ cup fresh mint leaves, cut into thin ribbons (see Charlie's Tip, page 241)

3 to 4 tablespoons balsamic glaze (see Charlie's Tip, page 218)

Flaky sea salt, such as Maldon, or other salt

Freshly ground black pepper

Place the arugula in an even layer on a large serving platter. Scatter the watermelon and tomatoes on top of the arugula. Sprinkle evenly with the feta and mint.

Drizzle with the balsamic glaze and season with flaky salt and pepper. Serve immediately.

· FOXHUNTING ·
ETIQUETTE

- *When riding on the road, remain to one side to allow cars to pass. Wave the cars by if they are unable to see traffic and acknowledge the passerby in some polite manner. If hounds are crossing the road or being hacked down the road, slow traffic down or stop if necessary.*

Coconut CHEESECAKE

—₩₩ *Makes one 9-inch cake* ₩₩—

FOR THE CRUST

Nonstick baking spray

⅔ cup roasted salted macadamia
  nuts, finely chopped

⅔ cup sweetened shredded coconut

⅔ cup graham cracker crumbs

¼ cup unrefined coconut oil, melted

FOR THE FILLING

3 (8-ounce) packages cream cheese,
  at room temperature

1 cup granulated sugar

3 large eggs, at room temperature

⅔ cup full-fat canned coconut milk,
  at room temperature

½ teaspoon pure vanilla extract

1½ teaspoons coconut extract

FOR THE TOPPING

1 cup heavy cream

2 tablespoons confectioners' sugar

1 teaspoon coconut extract

¾ to 1 cup large coconut flakes,
  lightly toasted (see Charlie's Tip)

Make the crust: Preheat the oven to 325°F. Position one oven rack in the center position and one in the lowest. On the lowest rack, place a baking pan filled with 1 inch of water. Spray a 9-inch springform pan with baking spray and wrap the outside of the pan with aluminum foil.

In a large bowl, stir together the nuts, shredded coconut, cracker crumbs, and coconut oil until thoroughly combined. Press the mixture evenly over the bottom of the prepared pan. Bake the crust for 12 to 14 minutes, until it just starts to brown around the edges. Remove from the oven and let cool completely in the pan set on a wire rack. Reduce the oven temperature to 300°F.

Make the filling: In a large bowl using a handheld mixer, beat the cream cheese on medium-high speed until smooth. Add the granulatd sugar and beat until the mixture becomes light and fluffy. Add the eggs one at a time, beating until thoroughly combined after each addition. Add the coconut milk, vanilla, and coconut extract and beat again until smooth. Pour the filling over the cooled crust.

Place the pan on the center rack of the oven. Bake for 1 hour 30 minutes, or until the edges are set but the center still jiggles slightly. Turn off the oven, wedge the oven door open with the handle of a wooden spoon, and let the cake cool for about 1 hour. (Cooling the cake slowly prevents cracks in the top.) Cover with plastic wrap and refrigerate for at least 4 hours or up to 24.

Make the topping: In a chilled bowl using a handheld mixer with chilled beaters, beat the cream, confectioners' sugar, and coconut extract until it holds stiff peaks.

To serve, run a sharp knife between the cake and the sides of the pan to loosen the cake. Release the sides of the springform pan and remove the ring. Spread the whipped cream topping evenly over the top of the cheesecake and sprinkle with the toasted coconut flakes.

CHARLIE'S TIP

Toasting coconut deepens the flavor and gives it a nice crispy texture that makes a beautiful golden (and tasty) topping for this dessert. To toast the coconut, preheat the oven to 350°F. Line a rimmed baking sheet with parchment paper. Spread the coconut evenly over the prepared baking sheet and toast in the oven, stirring occasionally, for 5 to 7 minutes, until golden brown. Coconut browns quickly in the oven, so keep an eye on it at all times. Remove from the oven and let cool.

THE HUNTSMAN'S GATHERING

Tangerine-Ginger Sparkler 248

Mâche Salad with French Vinaigrette 249

Goat Cheese & Herb–Stuffed Piquanté Peppers 250

Pasta with Pancetta & Peas 253

Southern Tomato Pie 256

Key Lime Pie 259

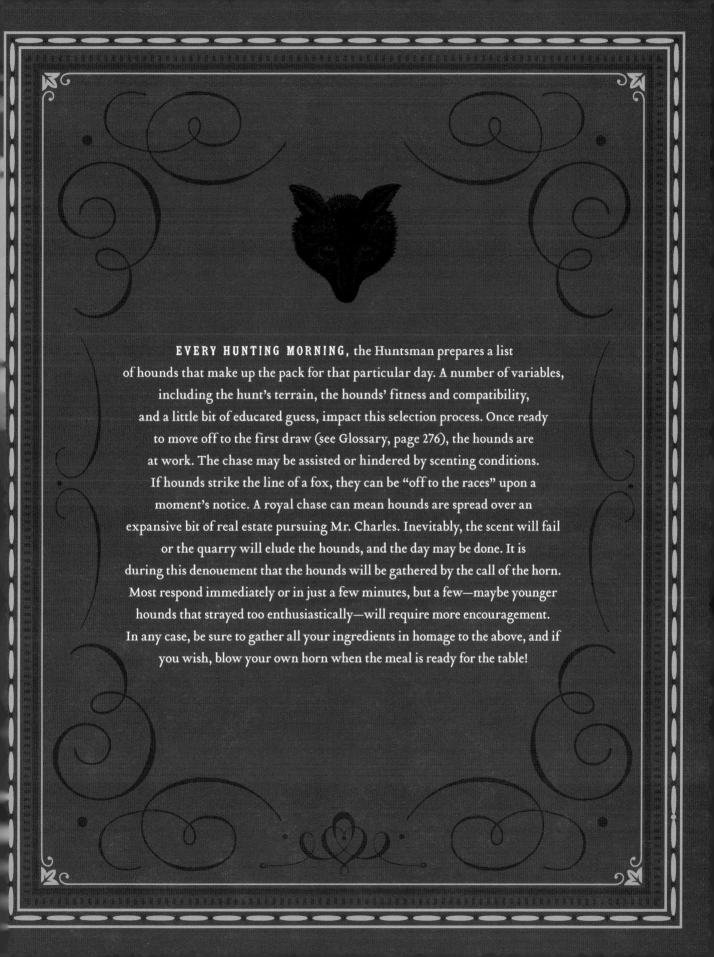

EVERY HUNTING MORNING, the Huntsman prepares a list
of hounds that make up the pack for that particular day. A number of variables,
including the hunt's terrain, the hounds' fitness and compatibility,
and a little bit of educated guess, impact this selection process. Once ready
to move off to the first draw (see Glossary, page 276), the hounds are
at work. The chase may be assisted or hindered by scenting conditions.
If hounds strike the line of a fox, they can be "off to the races" upon a
moment's notice. A royal chase can mean hounds are spread over an
expansive bit of real estate pursuing Mr. Charles. Inevitably, the scent will fail
or the quarry will elude the hounds, and the day may be done. It is
during this denouement that the hounds will be gathered by the call of the horn.
Most respond immediately or in just a few minutes, but a few—maybe younger
hounds that strayed too enthusiastically—will require more encouragement.
In any case, be sure to gather all your ingredients in homage to the above, and if
you wish, blow your own horn when the meal is ready for the table!

Tangerine-Ginger SPARKLER

⚜ Makes 1 drink ⚜

1 tablespoon Tangerine-Ginger
Syrup (recipe follows)

Prosecco or other sparkling wine

Pour the Tangerine-Ginger Syrup into a champagne flute and top with the prosecco or other sparkling wine. Serve immediately.

TANGERINE-GINGER SYRUP

Makes 1 cup

2 cups fresh tangerine juice (from
about 8 tangerines)

½ cup sugar
4 teaspoons chopped fresh ginger

In a medium saucepan, combine the tangerine juice, sugar, and ginger. Bring the mixture to a boil over medium-high heat and simmer for about 2 minutes, or until the sugar has dissolved. Remove the pan from the heat and let the mixture cool. Cover and refrigerate for a few hours or preferably overnight.

Strain the syrup through a fine-mesh sieve and discard the ginger. Store in an airtight container in the refrigerator for up to 3 weeks.

MÂCHE SALAD

WITH FRENCH VINAIGRETTE

⚞ Serves 6 ⚟

1 egg yolk

1 teaspoon Dijon mustard

1 tablespoon red wine vinegar

¼ cup extra-virgin olive oil

Sea salt and freshly ground black pepper

3 or 4 heads mâche lettuce or other soft lettuce, such as Bibb or Boston, torn into bite-size pieces

In a small bowl, whisk together the egg yolk, mustard, and vinegar. While whisking, slowly stream in the olive oil and whisk until emulsified (alternatively, emulsify the dressing using an immersion blender). Season with salt and pepper.

Place the lettuce in a large salad bowl and drizzle with the dressing. Toss to coat. Taste and season with salt and pepper as needed. Serve immediately.

- *Never leave the hunt without notifying the Field Master that you are dropping out. The Field Master will tell you the best way to return without interfering with the hunt. Before you hack back to the stable, trailer, or van, be sure to thank the Master, Field Master, and staff for a good day's sport.*

Goat Cheese & Herb–Stuffed
PIQUANTÉ PEPPERS

Makes 45 peppers

1 (14-ounce) jar sweet piquanté peppers (see Charlie's Tip)

8 ounces goat cheese

1 cup mixed fresh herbs, such as basil, thyme, lavender, and/or parsley

2 teaspoons extra-virgin olive oil

½ teaspoon sea salt

Drain the peppers in a colander and dry them between two dish towels. You want to remove as much moisture as possible.

In a food processor, combine the goat cheese, herbs, olive oil, and salt and process until smooth. Transfer the cheese spread to a piping bag. (Alternatively, transfer it to a plastic zip-top bag and snip off a small corner, or use a spoon to fill the peppers.) Fill each pepper with the cheese spread. Place the peppers on a serving platter, cover with plastic wrap, and refrigerate until ready to serve.

CHARLIE'S TIP

The sweet piquanté peppers we use in this recipe are small, red, and about the size of a cherry tomato. Originating from South Africa, these peppers are most commonly sold pickled in jars, often under the brand name Peppadew. They can be filled a few hours in advance and refrigerated. Bring them to room temperature before serving.

If you have leftover cheese spread, serve it with crackers, use it in place of butter when serving warm corn on the cob, or toss it with warm pasta.

PASTA
WITH PANCETTA & PEAS

Serves 6

1 tablespoon sea salt, plus more to taste

3 tablespoons unsalted butter

½ pound pancetta, diced

1 white onion, finely diced

3 garlic cloves, crushed

⅓ cup heavy cream

1 pound fettuccine or tagliatelle

1½ cups cooked fresh peas

1½ cups coarsely grated Pecorino Romano or Parmesan cheese, plus more for serving

Freshly ground black pepper

Bring a large pot of water and 1 tablespoon salt to a boil.

Meanwhile, in a large skillet, melt 1 tablespoon of the butter over medium-high heat. Add the pancetta and cook until crisp and golden, about 6 minutes. Transfer the pancetta to a plate and set aside.

Melt the remaining 2 tablespoons butter in the skillet. Add the onion and garlic and cook, stirring, until translucent, about 8 minutes. Add the cream and bring the mixture to a simmer, stirring occasionally. Cook for a few minutes, until the mixture thickens to coat the back of a spoon.

Add the pasta to the boiling water and cook according to the package directions until just al dente. Drain well. Using tongs, transfer the pasta to the skillet with the cream sauce. Sprinkle with the pancetta, peas, and cheese and use the tongs to toss until all the pasta is coated. Season with salt and pepper.

Serve immediately, with extra cheese on the side.

The Laurels Preserve, Brandywine Conservancy

Southern
TOMATO PIE

~ Serves 8 ~

1 store-bought refrigerated piecrust

1½ pounds ripe red tomatoes, seeded and cut into ½-inch-thick slices

1 teaspoon sea salt

1 cup mayonnaise

1 cup shredded cheddar cheese

12 fresh basil leaves, coarsely chopped

Freshly ground black pepper

1 cup thinly sliced Vidalia onions

Preheat the oven to 400°F. Let the piecrust sit at room temperature for 15 minutes.

Unroll the piecrust and place it in a 9-inch deep-dish pie pan, gently pressing it into the bottom and up the sides of the dish. Using your fingers or a fork, crimp or flute the edge of the crust. Using a fork, prick the dough all over. Line the dough with parchment paper and fill the paper with dried beans or pie weights. Bake the crust for 20 minutes. Remove the beans or weights and parchment and let the crust cool. Reduce the oven temperature to 350°F.

Place the tomato slices in a large, shallow bowl and sprinkle with salt. Set aside for 15 minutes, allowing the excess juices to leach out.

Meanwhile, in a medium bowl, stir together the mayonnaise, cheese, basil, and pepper to taste.

Line the bottom of the parbaked crust with half the tomato slices, followed by all the onions in an even layer. Top with the remaining tomatoes. Spoon the cheese mixture over the top and smooth it out, leaving a small border uncovered just near the edge.

Wrap the crust with a foil collar (see Charlie's Tip) and bake for 20 minutes. Remove the collar and bake for another 20 to 25 minutes, until the cheese is golden brown, for a total baking time of 40 to 45 minutes. Remove from the oven and let cool for 30 minutes.

Serve warm or at room temperature.

CHARLIE'S TIP

*We like to make foil collars for piecrusts because it prevents them from burning.
(Pie guards, rings, or shields can be purchased as well.) To make one, simply take small strips of
aluminum foil and wrap them around the edge of the crust. If you want to get fancy, you can cut
an 11-inch circle from foil, then cut out the center to make your own "pie ring."*

Key Lime Pie with
Tangerine–Ginger Sparklers
(page 248)

KEY LIME PIE

~ Makes one 9-inch pie ~

FOR THE CRUST

Nonstick baking spray

2 cups graham cracker crumbs

¼ cup sugar

1 cup sweetened flaked coconut

½ cup (1 stick) salted butter, melted

FOR THE FILLING

1 (14-ounce) can sweetened condensed milk

Zest of 2 key limes

½ cup key lime juice (from 12 to 15 limes)

3 large egg yolks

¼ cup cold buttermilk

Whipped cream, for serving

Make the crust: Preheat the oven to 325°F. Lightly spray a 9-inch pie plate with baking spray.

In a medium bowl, stir together the cracker crumbs, sugar, and coconut until thoroughly combined. Add the butter and stir until the mixture is thoroughly moistened. Press the mixture over the bottom and up the sides of the prepared pie plate. Set aside.

Make the filling: In a medium bowl, whisk together the condensed milk, lime zest, and lime juice.

In a large bowl using a handheld mixer, beat the egg yolks on high speed for 4 to 5 minutes, until the yolks are pale and ribbons form when the beaters are lifted out. Gradually whisk in the condensed milk mixture until thoroughly combined. Pour in the buttermilk and stir to combine.

Pour the filling into the crust. Bake for 20 to 25 minutes, until the filling is set around the edges but still slightly jiggly. Transfer to a wire rack to cool for 1 hour. Cover the pie with plastic wrap lightly greased with baking spray and freeze for 4 to 6 hours.

Slice and serve with a dollop of whipped cream if desired.

MENU FIFTEEN

CUBBING SUMMER SUPPER

Moscow Mule 263

Curried Crab Cakes 264

Tortellini Chicken Alfredo 267

Farmers' Market Succotash 268

Boone Salad 271

Fox Gingerbread Cookies 272

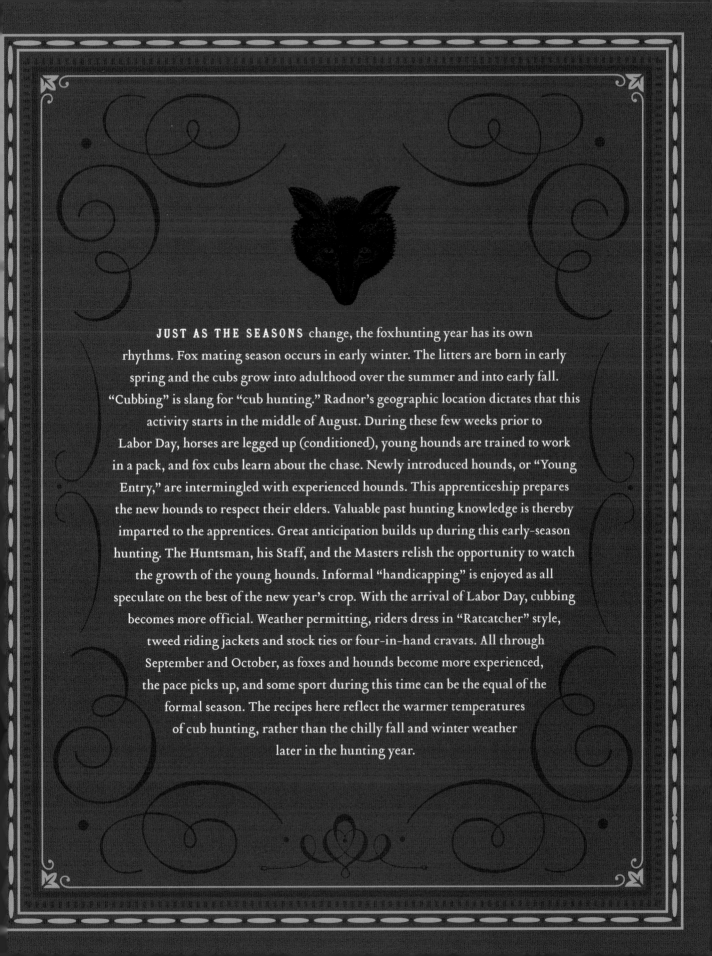

JUST AS THE SEASONS change, the foxhunting year has its own
rhythms. Fox mating season occurs in early winter. The litters are born in early
spring and the cubs grow into adulthood over the summer and into early fall.
"Cubbing" is slang for "cub hunting." Radnor's geographic location dictates that this
activity starts in the middle of August. During these few weeks prior to
Labor Day, horses are legged up (conditioned), young hounds are trained to work
in a pack, and fox cubs learn about the chase. Newly introduced hounds, or "Young
Entry," are intermingled with experienced hounds. This apprenticeship prepares
the new hounds to respect their elders. Valuable past hunting knowledge is thereby
imparted to the apprentices. Great anticipation builds up during this early-season
hunting. The Huntsman, his Staff, and the Masters relish the opportunity to watch
the growth of the young hounds. Informal "handicapping" is enjoyed as all
speculate on the best of the new year's crop. With the arrival of Labor Day, cubbing
becomes more official. Weather permitting, riders dress in "Ratcatcher" style,
tweed riding jackets and stock ties or four-in-hand cravats. All through
September and October, as foxes and hounds become more experienced,
the pace picks up, and some sport during this time can be the equal of the
formal season. The recipes here reflect the warmer temperatures
of cub hunting, rather than the chilly fall and winter weather
later in the hunting year.

Moscow Mules with Curried Crab Cakes (page 264)

MOSCOW MULE

Makes 1 drink

Handful of ice

2 ounces vodka

1 ounce fresh lime juice (from about 1 lime)

4 to 6 ounces good-quality ginger beer

Lime wedge, for garnish

Fill a copper mug or highball glass with ice. Pour in the vodka and lime juice and top with the ginger beer. Stir. Garnish with the lime wedge and serve immediately.

· FOXHUNTING · **ETIQUETTE**

- *Cub hunting attire is less formal than regular season attire, mainly because the weather still tends to be warm. A collared shirt of subdued hue (polo, ladies' show shirt, or gentleman's dress shirt with tie), breeches (traditionally tan, gray, brown, or rust-colored), and black or brown high boots are acceptable, as are similarly colored jodhpurs and "paddock" or jodhpur boots. Hard hats may be brown, gray, or black. (Note that in the United States, ribbon tails on hard hats should run upward; downward is reserved for professional staff.) The ensemble should be completed with a tweed jacket or linen jacket, although this requirement is waived in September if the weather is too uncomfortably warm for jackets.*

Curried
CRAB CAKES

Makes 14 crab cakes

1 large egg, beaten

¼ cup mayonnaise

½ teaspoon sea salt

½ teaspoon Old Bay seasoning

1½ teaspoons curry powder

1 teaspoon dry mustard

1 pound lump crabmeat

¼ cup Italian breadcrumbs

2 tablespoons unsalted butter

2 tablespoons extra-virgin olive oil, plus more as needed

Mango chutney, for serving

Small fresh cilantro leaves, for garnish

Preheat the oven to 250°F. Line a rimmed baking sheet with parchment paper.

In a large bowl, whisk together the egg, mayonnaise, salt, Old Bay, curry powder, and dry mustard until smooth. Add the crab and breadcrumbs and gently toss to combine. Shape the mixture into 2-tablespoon mounds and place them on the baking sheet.

In a large skillet, heat the butter and oil over medium heat until the butter has melted. Working in batches to avoid crowding the pan, use a spatula to gently slide the crab cakes into the pan and fry for about 3 minutes per side. Add more oil to the pan as needed if it becomes dry. Transfer the fried crab cakes back to the baking sheet and keep warm in the oven until ready to serve.

Just before serving, top each crab cake with a dollop of mango chutney, and garnish with a small cilantro leaf.

Tortellini
CHICKEN ALFREDO

⧼ Serves 4 ⧽

4 teaspoons sea salt

1 pound fresh tortellini

2 tablespoons extra-virgin olive oil

2 boneless, skinless chicken breasts, cut into small cubes

4 tablespoons (½ stick) unsalted butter

¼ pound prosciutto, diced

1 cup fresh spinach

½ cup mushrooms, finely chopped

2 cups heavy cream

2 cups coarsely grated Parmesan cheese (about 8 ounces), plus more for serving

1 cup cooked peas

1 teaspoon dried oregano

1 teaspoon chopped fresh parsley

¼ teaspoon freshly ground black pepper

1 teaspoon garlic powder

Fill a large pot with water and add 1 tablespoon of the salt. Bring the water to a boil over high heat. Add the tortellini and cook according to the package directions. Drain and set aside.

In a large skillet, heat the olive oil over medium-high heat until it shimmers. Add the chicken and cook, stirring, until browned and cooked through, 6 to 8 minutes. Transfer the chicken to a plate and set aside.

In the same skillet, melt the butter over medium heat. Add the prosciutto and cook, stirring, for 2 minutes. Add the spinach and mushrooms and cook for 2 minutes more. Pour in the cream and simmer until reduced by half. While stirring continuously, slowly add the cheese and the remaining teaspoon salt until the sauce is thickened to the consistency of buttermilk and smooth. You may not need to use all the cheese—reserve any remaining cheese for serving. Stir in the peas, chicken (and any juices that have accumulated on the plate), tortellini, oregano, parsley, pepper, and garlic powder.

Serve with extra cheese.

Farmers' Market
SUCCOTASH

❦ Serves 4 to 6 ❦

2 tablespoons extra-virgin olive oil

1 large onion, chopped

1 large garlic clove, minced

8 plum tomatoes, coarsely chopped

Fresh corn kernels cut from 4 ears of corn (about 2 ¼ cups)

2 cups fresh lima beans

Sea salt and freshly ground black pepper to taste

3 tablespoons thinly sliced fresh basil (see Charlie's Tip, page 241)

In a large pot, heat the oil over medium heat until it shimmers. Add the onion and cook for 8 minutes, or until it becomes soft and translucent. Stir in the garlic, and cook until fragrant, about 1 minute. Add the tomatoes, corn, and lima beans and stir to combine. Reduce the heat to medium-low, cover, and simmer, stirring occasionally, until the corn and lima beans are tender and the tomatoes are soft, 20 to 30 minutes. Season with salt and pepper to taste.

Stir in the basil just before serving.

BOONE SALAD

≈ Serves 8 ≈

12 ripe red tomatoes, cut into
    1-inch-thick wedges

1 tablespoon sea salt, plus more to
    taste

1 cup extra-virgin olive oil

2 cups fresh basil leaves, cut into
    thin ribbons (see Charlie's Tip,
    page 241)

1 large red onion, thinly sliced

1 yellow bell pepper, cut into thin
    strips

1 red bell pepper, cut into thin strips

1 orange bell pepper, cut into thin
    strips

2 to 3 tablespoons white balsamic
    vinegar

Freshly ground black pepper

French bread, for serving

In a large wooden bowl, combine the tomatoes and salt and let stand at room temperature for 1 hour. Stir in ½ cup of the olive oil and let stand for 2 to 3 hours more.

Add the basil, onion, bell peppers, vinegar, and remaining ½ cup olive oil and toss to combine. Let the mixture marinate for 1 hour more, stirring occasionally. Season with salt and pepper.

Serve with French bread for dipping into the sauce.

CHARLIE'S TIP

*If you have leftover salad, it makes wonderful gazpacho. The next day,
simply put the leftover salad in a food processor and add 2 to 3 tablespoons olive oil and
1 teaspoon balsamic vinegar. Blend, but don't puree until smooth—the gazpacho should be
chunky. Serve with a dollop of sour cream and a basil leaf for garnish.*

Fox
GINGERBREAD COOKIES

✦ Makes 2 dozen 4-inch cookies ✦

3 cups all-purpose flour

1½ teaspoons baking powder

1 teaspoon baking soda

¼ teaspoon sea salt

1 tablespoon ground ginger

½ teaspoon ground cinnamon

½ teaspoon ground allspice

6 tablespoons (¾ stick) unsalted butter, at room temperature

¾ cup packed dark brown sugar

1 large egg

½ cup molasses

1 teaspoon pure vanilla extract

Icing of your choice

In a medium bowl, stir together the flour, baking powder, baking soda, salt, ginger, cinnamon, and allspice.

In a large bowl using a handheld mixer, beat the butter, brown sugar, and egg on medium speed until well blended. Add the molasses and vanilla. Gradually stir in the dry ingredients and mix until smooth. (Alternatively, you can make this dough in a food processor.)

Divide the dough in half. Wrap each portion in plastic and let stand at room temperature for 2 hours. (The dough can be made up to 4 days in advance and refrigerated. Bring the dough to room temperature before using.)

Preheat the oven to 375°F. Line two rimmed baking sheets with parchment paper.

On a lightly floured work surface, use a floured rolling pin to roll out the dough to a scant ¼-inch thickness. Cut out cookies with desired cutters and place them 1 inch apart on the prepared baking sheet.

Bake for 7 to 10 minutes (less time equals a softer cookie). Remove from the oven and let cool on the baking sheet for 10 minutes, then transfer to a wire rack to cool completely.

Decorate the cooled cookies with your favorite icing.

Bryn Coed Preserve, Natural Lands

Glossary

OF HUNTING TERMS & PHRASES

AWAY (adv.) A fox has "gone away" when he has left covert (see opposite). Hounds are "away" when they have left covert on the line of a fox.

BABBLE (v.) To give tongue on a scent other than fox, on no scent at all, or on a scent too faint to follow.

BLANK (n.) To draw blank is to fail to find a fox.

BITCH 1. (n.) A female foxhound. 2. (v.) What the field does when the weather, footing, scent, etc., isn't good.

BRUSH (n.) A fox's tail is always called a brush.

CAST 1. (n.) A planned move in searching for a new or lost line (see page 278); To make a cast. 2. (n.) Hounds may cast themselves, or the Huntsman may cast them.

CHECK 1. (n.) An interruption of the run caused by hounds losing the line. 2. (v.) Hounds check when they lose the line temporarily.

COLORS (n.) The distinctive colors that distinguish the uniform of one hunt from another. Usually a distinctive collar color on a scarlet coat, however, some hunts have coats other than scarlet. To be awarded colors is to be given the right to wear them and the hunt button, signifying a level of seniority and competence in the field.

COUPLE 1. (n.) Two hounds (any sex), for convenience in counting. 2. (n.) A device for keeping two hounds attached to each other for convenience in control or training. 3. (v.) To attach two hounds together by use of couples.

COVERT (pronounced "cover"; n.) A patch of woods or brush where a fox might be found.

CRY (n.) The sound given by hounds when hunting; e.g., "The pack in full cry."

CUB 1. (n.) A young fox. 2. (n.) Hunting (colloquially, "cubbing"). Early hunting before the formal season. Hounds are encouraged to stay in covert, foxes that go away being permitted to do so in peace if practical. This gets cubs in the habit of running straight, rather than circling in the covert.

DOG (n.) A male foxhound. (Packs are correctly called hounds or foxhounds and not called dogs unless they are all male.)

DOUBLE (v.) To "double the horn" is to blow a series of short sharp notes, signifying a fox is afoot. The "gone away" note is a form of "doubling the horn."

DOUBLE BACK (v.) A fox that returns to covert after having left it is said to double back.

DRAW 1. (v.) To search for a fox in a certain area; e.g., "To draw a covert." 2. (n.) The act of drawing; e.g., "Thorny Wood is a difficult draw." 3. (v.) To select and separate a hound or a group of hounds in kennels for a particular purpose; e.g., "Please draw out Bluebell's last year's litter, so I can show them to Mr. Jones."

DRIVE (n.) The urge to get forward well with the line; e.g., "That hound has drive."

DWELL (v.) To hunt without getting forward. A hound that lacks drive is apt to dwell.

EARTH (n.) Any place where a fox goes to ground for protection, but usually a place where foxes live regularly; a fox den.

ENTER (v.) A hound is entered when he is first regularly used for hunting. "This year's entry'" are the hounds entered or to be entered this season.

FEATHER (v.) When a hound indicates by actions, rather than by voice, that he is on a line or near it. The stern is waved, and activity is concentrated and intensified.

FIELD (n.) The group of people riding to hounds, excluding the Master of Foxhounds and staff. When feasible (primarily in the Radnor home country), there is a "jumping over obstacles—such as a fence or wall" field and a "non-jumping over obstacles" field.

FIELD MASTER (n.) The person designated to control the field by the Master of Foxhounds.

FIXTURE (n.) The time and place of the meet or assembly of the hunt. A fixture card is a card sent out to list the fixtures for a given period.

FOX CHASING (n.) The correct term for the American sport commonly called foxhunting. As it is not our objective, nor generally our practice, to kill the quarry, foxhunting is technically "fox chasing," and is referenced as such by the Pennsylvania Game Commission, among others.

GROUND (n./v.) To take shelter (usually underground) or to go to ground; e.g., "The fox went to ground in the drain."

HEAD (v.) To cause a fox to turn from its planned direction of travel. This usually causes a check and is not recommended.

HEEL (adv.) Backward. Hounds following the line the wrong way are running heel (also called "counter").

HOLD HARD (n./v.) "Stop, please." If used twice to the same individual, it probably means "Stop, please, damn you."

HONOR (v.) When a hound gives tongue on a line that another hound has been hunting.

HUNTSMAN (n.) The person who controls hounds in the field.

KENNELMEN (n.) He/she who takes care of hounds and kennels.

LARK (v.) To jump fences unnecessarily when hounds are not running or on non-hunting days. (This annoys landowners and is not recommended.)

LIFT (v.) To carry hounds forward, implying that hounds were hunting when lifted. (It's risky but sometimes advisable.)

LINE (n.) The trail of the fox.

LITTER (n.) A group of young born of the same mother at the same time. In foxhunting, this applies to whelps (see opposite) or fox cubs.

MALVERN (n.) The Radnor Clubhouse has been located in Malvern, Pennsylvania, since 1931.

MARK (v.) When a hound indicates that a fox has gone to ground. He stops at the earth, tries to dig his way in, and gives tongue in a way quite different from his hunting voice. Some hounds are better at marking than others.

MASTER (n.) The Master of Foxhounds (MFH) is the person in command of the hunt in field and kennels.

MEET (n./v.) The assembling of the hunt for a day's sport; e.g., "The meet tomorrow is early" or "Hounds meet tomorrow at noon"

NOSE (n.) The ability of a hound to detect and interpret the scent.

OPEN (v.) When a hound first gives tongue on a line.

PAD 1. (n.) The foot of a fox. 2. (n.) The center cushion of a hound's foot.

PANEL 1. (n.) The portion of any jumpable fence between two posts. 2. (n.) A jumpable portion built into a wire fence.

POINT 1. (n.) The straight line distance made good in a run; e.g., "That was a six-mile point, but twelve miles as hounds run." 2. (n.) The location to which a Whipper-In is sent to watch for a fox to go away.

RATE (n.) A warning cry given to correct hounds; e.g., "Back to him" or "Ware riot." The word is less important than the intonation.

RIOT (n.) Anything that hounds might hunt that they shouldn't (often deer).

RUN (n.) A period during which hounds are actually hunting on the line of a fox. (It usually implies a gallop for the field, as opposed to a hunt in covert after a twisting fox.)

SCENT (n.) The smell of a fox, and the physical and chemical phenomena by which the smell gets from the fox's footprints to the hound's nose. Scent can be good or bad, meaning easy to follow or difficult, depending, in general, on the weather. Fox scent is similar to that of skunk, but not as acrid.

SPEAK (v.) To give tongue. (It is usually of a single hound; e.g., "I heard old Homer open, and he spoke for some time before the others got to him.")

STAFF (n.) The Huntsman and Whippers-In.

STERN (n.) The tail of a hound.

TONGUE 1. (n.) Cry. A hound "gives tongue" when he proclaims with his voice that he is on a line. 2. (v.) To give tongue.

VIEW 1. (v.) To see the fox. 2. (n.) The sight of the fox.

VIEW HOLLOA (n.) The cry given by a staff member on viewing a fox.

WHELP 1. (n.) A young puppy. 2. (v.) To bear puppies; e.g., "That hound was whelped 3/6/02."

WHIPPER-IN/WHIPPERS-IN (n.) A staff member who assists the Huntsman in control of hounds.

Acknowledgments

I'd like to extend a BIG THANKS to all of you who helped with this extensive project! It took so many to produce this work, including many who aren't even named here. I am grateful to each and every one of you!

I'D LIKE TO EXTEND MY DEEPEST APPRECIATION TO:

The MASTERS OF THE HUNT, Mike Tillson, Collin McNeil, Esther Gansky, and Wes Hardin, who let me run with this fund-raising idea more than a year ago.

LISA DAVNE and NICOLE RIEGL, my recipe curators, whose expertise was invaluable. Their organizing, testing, vetting, and acting as sous chefs for the photo shoots made this project possible! I was so impressed!

ALEX WARZECHA, Hunt Secretary, the computer wizard, for formatting all my needs for this project without one complaint. You're the best!

ALICIA SCHROER, whom I relied on for insight, not only at the production meetings in New York City, but also at the photo shoots and the rendezvous at my house going over the passes of the cookbook. I so enjoyed your company!

EILEEN CORL, Club President, for your willingness to always help—and for being my voice outside of the committee and to the rest of the CLUB MEMBERSHIP!

HELEN SIPALA, my first recruit and generous donor to the auction fund-raisers.

All of our SPONSORS, especially the Moran family, who generously backed the book with a dedication to their mother, Betty Moran!

Thanks also to our FIRST DONORS, JUDY and DON ROSATO.

MARIPEG BRUDER, for understanding the importance of underwriting the history chapter of the Club.

My fabulous COOKBOOK COMMITTEE, who generously gave their time and talent to keep this project going for well over a year: Georgia Brutscher, Maggie Cappelli, Eileen Corl, Tracey Costello, Lisa Davne, Esther Gansky, Barbara Hill, Patsy Jones, Anna Kreuzberger, Collin McNeil, Janice Murdoch, Meggin Patterson, Stevi Richards, Nicole Riegl, Judy Rosato, Alicia Schroer, Helen Sipala, and Alex Warzecha.

Radnor Hunt's CHEF TYLER TURNER, who supported this project and graciously shared his personal recipes with us.

All the COOKS, BAKERS, and MIXOLOGISTS who prepared the recipes—and the willing TESTERS who sampled them.

The DAVNES and PATTERSONS, who hosted tasting parties and ignited enthusiasm for the book.

TRACEY COSTELLO, who helped organize the tasting and launch parties.

ESTHER GANSKY and her husband PAUL, who shared their fabulous hunting curios and memorabilia for the photo shoots.

The extended family of SUPPORTERS who helped with fund-raising: Bunny Meister, Sharon Vinton, Kathy Craven, Angi Bevers, Betsy Stefferud, Clifford Carver, Rebekah Robinson, Katie Call, and Cindy Connors. I can't thank you enough!

To our Huntsman, JOHN DEAN, for taking such good care of the Hounds and helping at the paper chase fund-raiser with his wife, NANCY.

WHITE HORSE WINERY, owned by BROCK and YVONNE VINTON and their son, BJ, who supplied the 2015 Vintner's Red, during a think tank, which provided liquid inspiration for me to come up with the title, *The Fox's Kitchen*.

My local SHOPS and BUSINESSES: A. J. Blosenski, Arader Tree Service, Archer & Buchanan Architecture, Barnyard Products, Gardner's Landscape & Nursery, Nuprint, Pickering Valley Feed & Farm Store, Ron's Original Bar & Grille, Synergy Sports & Corrective Massage, LLC , and Walter J. Cook Jeweler.

BARB KING, owner of VALLEY FORGE FLOWERS, for hosting the launch party in her fabulous barn store and providing the table setting for the Spring Fling chapter opener.

BOOTH MALONE and ELISE PHILLIPS, for donating an original piece of artwork to our fund-raiser.

TRISH HUEBER, whose premature passing was a shock to all. We wish you were here to see the cookbook realized.

KATHIE FRIEDENBERG, our in-house sculptor, who gave us permission to use an image of one of her pieces.

CONSERVATION GROUPS—Brandywine Conservancy, Brandywine Red Clay Alliance, Cheshire Land Preservation Fund, French & Pickering Creeks Conservation Trust, Natural Lands, and Willistown Conservation Trust—who help preserve the land we all enjoy.

And to the CHESTER COUNTY HISTORICAL SOCIETY and GREENER PARTNERS, for having such a positive impact in the area and the people who live here.

My MOM and DAD, for giving me the skills and fortitude to tackle this big project.

MY FAMILY, for losing a year of Mommy to her desk and cookbook fund-raisers.

And to my husband, COLLIN MCNEIL— my in-house scribe for his inspired words included in the book, from the introduction to the chapter openers— and for being the best husband one could ever hope for!

TO THE PROFESSIONALS—YOU ARE QUITE A TEAM!

Our publisher, DERRYDALE PRESS, and AMY LYONS, who were enthusiastic from the get-go.

LAURA PALESE, an unbelievable creative force who crafted the perfect design.

BRIAN DONNELLY, whose spectacular photographs brought the recipes to life and showed off the magnificent conserved countryside.

REBECCA FFRENCH, our endlessly enthusiastic production manager, who ensured the many pieces and people worked together to produce the best cookbook we could. It wouldn't have become what it is without you!

DAN MACEY, our food stylist, who made every recipe deliciously camera-ready.

FOUR COLOUR PRINT GROUP, for ensuring the book would dazzle.

Horse, hound, and Virginia McNeil

DARIA KILLINGER/EQUISCAPE, for sharing her years of foxhunting images.

GENEVIEVE SNYDER, for sharing her wonderful hunting images.

MICHAEL DEHAVEN with **RAINER & CO.**, for keeping our books in order.

BRITT MURDOCH, FRANK LETO, and **AL MURPHY** with **BRYN MAWR TRUST**, for providing all our banking needs on such a personal level.

RICH CAPUTO with **FOX ROTHSCHILD**, whose capable hands helped us to bring The Hounds Foundation to life.

ERIN DOUGHERTY, for doing everything so efficiently and with a smile.

I'd also like to extend a huge thanks to all the following **CLUB MEMBERS** and **FRIENDS** who submitted recipes. We wish we could have included everyone's recipes, but our menus were limited: Skip Abbott, Alaina Alexander, Marjorie Allen, Carol Atterbury, Betsy Bacon, Jan Beale, Angi Bevers, Maripeg Bruder, Georgia Brutscher, Claudia Caldwell, Eric Corkhill, Tracey Costello, Carol Cropper, Lisa Davne, Megan Freeman, Esther Gansky, Jean Good, Christina Graham, Kirk Harman, Barbara Hill, Jeana Hollands, Trish Hueber, Patsy Jones, Barbara Keough, Anna Kreuzberger, Leslie Lindsley, Dan Macey, Peggy Matje, John B. McGowan, Jr., Debbie McKechnie, Leanne McMenamin, Collin McNeil, Hillary Meisel, Carole Nevin, Robin Newman, Charles Nichols, Allison Patterson, Meggin Patterson, Blaire Baron Pew, Stevi Richards, Ed Riegl, Nicole Riegl, Megan Rohr, Don Rosato, Judy Rosato, Christa Schmidt, Alicia Schroer, Helen Sipala, MaryAnn Thompson, Heather Trish, Tyler Turner, Sharon Vinton, Yvonne Vinton, Cortie Wetherill, Janice Wetherill, Sonja White.

—VIRGINIA JUDSON MCNEIL,
*Radnor Hunt Cookbook
Committee Chairman, 2018*

INDEX

Page numbers in *italics* indicate illustrations

Aïoli, Sriracha, 191

alcohol, cooking with, 92

Almond Poppy Seed Cake with Balsamic Berries, 210

Almonds, Cocoa Espresso Cardamom, 101

appetizers & soups. *See also* bites; dips & spreads
Creamy Mushroom Tart, 157
Creole Shrimp, 180
Golden Mushroom Soup, 119
Moroccan Lamb Lettuce Cups, 202
Retro Molded Egg Salad Appetizer, 65
Southern Tomato Pie, 256
Sweet Potato & Chestnut Soup, 87
Tomato, Cannellini & Rosemary Soup, 33
Truffle Pizza, 138

Apple Cider Rumtini, 130

Apricot & Horseradish Sauce, 188

art & artifacts at Radnor Hunt, *36, 49, 129, 151, 234–35*

Artichoke & Caper Dip, 51

Arugula, Prosciutto & Provolone Rolls, 238

Arugula, Watermelon & Feta Salad, 242

Arugula & Macadamia Salad with Green Goddess Dressing, 34

Asparagus with Hazelnuts & Tarragon Vinaigrette, 209

Balsamic Berries, 210

balsamic glaze & vinegar, 218

Bananas Foster Cheesecake, 93

Beale, Edward, 16, *18*

Béarnaise Sauce, 176

Beer Cheese, 134

Belgian Beef Stew, 158

beverages
Apple Cider Rumtini, 130
Blackberry-Rosemary Rum Cocktail, 26
Classic Whiskey Sour, 154
Cucumber Water, 233
Cucumber-Ginger Margarita, 230
Devon Julep, 200
Earl Grey Gin & Tonic, 186
Earl Grey–Infused Gin, 186
Homemade Coffee Liqueur, 126
Lemonade, 48
Moscow Mule, 263
The Perfect Rob Roy, 84
Planter's Punch, 62
Polo Punch, 48
Pomegranate-Rosemary Gin Cocktail, 217
Rosemary Maple Bourbon Sour, 98
Spicy Bloody Mary, 168
Tangerine-Ginger Sparkler, 248
White Russian Cocktail, 126–27

bites
Blue Cheese Pecans, 133
Cocoa Espresso Cardamom Almonds, 101
Curried Crab Cakes, 264
Fried Zucchini Ribbons with Tzatziki, 236
Goat Cheese & Herb–Stuffed Piquanté Peppers, 250
Green Bean Fries, 146
Grilled Peaches with Serrano Ham, 218
Homemade Dill Pickles, 171
Prosciutto, Arugula & Provolone Rolls, 238
Scotch Eggs, 137
Seared Sesame Tuna Bites, 102
Sweet & Spicy Mixed Nuts, 29

Blackberry-Rosemary Rum Cocktail, 26

Blackberry-Rosemary Syrup, 26

Bloody Mary, Spicy, 168

Blue Cheese Pecans, 133

Boone Salad, 271

bouquet garni, 107

Bourbon Chocolate Pecan Bread Pudding, 149

Bourbon Sour, Rosemary Maple, 98

Braised–Red Wine Short Ribs, 122

Brandywine Conservancy, 7, *254–55*

Brandywine Red Clay Alliance, 7, *120–21*

Bread Pudding, Chocolate Bourbon Pecan, 149

breadcrumbs, homemade, 125

Broccolini with Lemon & Garlic, 88

broken Béarnaise or Hollandaise sauce, 177

Brown Sugar–Rosemary Syrup, 217

Brownies, Caramel & Sea Salt, 77

Brussels Sprout Salad with Mustard Vinaigrette, 162

Brussels Sprouts, Roasted, with Bacon & Sriracha Aïoli, 191

Bryn Coed Preserve, *274–75*

Bryn Mawr Hound Show, *203*

Buttermilk Glaze, 42

Cabbage, Clementines & Romaine Salad, 104

cakes & frostings
Bananas Foster Cheesecake, 93
Buttermilk Glaze, 42
Candied Carrot Cake, 42
Coconut Cheesecake, 244
Cream Cheese Frosting, 42
Gluten-Free Walnut Rosemary Coconut Cake, 225
Malted Milk Ball Cake, 163
Poppy Seed Almond Cake with Balsamic Berries, 210
Sour Cream Coffee Cake, 183

Calypso Turkey Sliders, 144

Candied Carrot Cake, 42

Cannellini, Tomato & Rosemary Soup, 33

Caper & Artichoke Dip, 51

Caper & Sun-Dried Tomato Tapenade, 116

Caramel & Sea Salt Brownies, 77

Caramel Sauce for Bread Pudding, 149, 150

Cardamom Cocoa Espresso Almonds, 101

Carrots au Gratin, 160

Cashew Chicken Chili, 73

Cauliflower, Roasted, with Hollandaise Sauce, 222

Charlie's Tips, 22, 29, 30, 33, 34, 48, 51, 66, 69, 70, 74, 81, 88, 91, 92, 101, 102, 107,

108, 125, 130, 133, 134, 142, 144, 147, 150, 162, 168, 177, 186, 188, 196, 203, 209, 213, 218, 221, 226, 237, 241, 245, 250, 257, 271
Cheshire Land Preservation Fund, 7, *112–13*
Chester County Historical Society, 7, *232*
Chestnut & Sweet Potato Soup, 87
Chicken, Hearty Skillet, 205
Chicken Alfredo Tortellini, 267
Chicken Cashew Chili, 73
chiffonade, 241
Chili, Chicken Cashew, 73
Chili, Venison, 143
Chocolate Bourbon Pecan Bread Pudding, 149
Chocolate Chip Pecan Oatmeal Cookies, 56
Chocolate Hazelnut Tart, Dark, 111
Chutney Cheese Pâté, 187
Classic Whiskey Sour, 154
Clementines, Cabbage & Romaine Salad, 104
cocktails. *See* beverages
Cocoa Espresso Cardamom Almonds, 101
Coconut Cheesecake, 244
Coconut Walnut Rosemary Cake, Gluten-Free, 225
Coffee Cake, Sour Cream, 183
Coffee Liqueur, Homemade, 126
cookies
    Caramel & Sea Salt Brownies, 77
    Chocolate Chip Pecan Oatmeal Cookies, 56
    English Flapjacks, 81
    Fox Gingerbread Cookies, 272
    Russian Tea Cakes, 196
cooking for a crowd. *See individual recipes*
Coq au Vin, 105
corn, fresh, 69
Corn & Saffron Risotto, 124
Corn Salad, Roasted, 70
Côte de Boeuf, 91
Cream Cheese Frosting, 42
Creamy Mushroom Tart, 157
Creole Shrimp, 180
Crickett Hill Farm, *194–95*
"cubbing" (cub hunting), 229, 261
Cucumber Water, 233
Cucumber-Ginger Margarita, 230
Curried Crab Cakes, 264
cutting herbs, (chiffonade) 241

Dark Chocolate Hazelnut Tart, 111
desserts. *See also* cakes & frostings; cookies
    Balsamic Berries, 210
    Chocolate Bourbon Pecan Bread Pudding, 149
    Dark Chocolate Hazelnut Tart, 111
    Key Lime Pie, 259
    Red Wine Sorbet, 92
    White Russian Cocktail, 126
Devon Julep, 200
Dill Pickles, Homemade, 171
dips & spreads
    Artichoke & Caper Dip, 51
    Beer Cheese, 134
    Chutney Cheese Pâté, 187
    Easy Fig Spread, 30
    Sun-Dried Tomato & Caper Tapenade, 116
    Texas Caviar Dip, 68
    Tzatziki, 236

Earl Grey Gin & Tonic, 186
Easy Summer Pasta, 241
Egg Salad Appetizer, Retro Molded, 65
Eggs, Poached, on Brioche with Spinach, Spicy Bacon & Béarnaise Sauce, 175
Eggs, Scotch, 137
English Flapjacks, 81
Espresso Cocoa Cardamom Almonds, 101
Evans, William, *19*

Farmers' Market Succotash, 268
Feta, Watermelon & Arugula, 242
Fig Spread, Easy, 30
Flapjacks, English, 81
foil collar to prevent burning, 257
Fox, Charles James, 22, *23*
Fox Gingerbread Cookies, 272
foxes, about, 22, 47, 83, 153, 261
foxhunting attire, 17, 25, 67, 97, 261, 263
foxhunting etiquette, 22, 37, 67, 78, 109, 116, 119, 159, 171, 180, 193, 200, 217, 230, 238, 242, 249, 263

foxhunting protocol & staffing, 21, 25, 37, 61, 109, 116, 153, 185, 215, 247. *See also* foxhunting etiquette
freezing cake, 213; soup, 33
French & Pickering Creeks Conservation Trust, 7, *194–95*
French Vinaigrette, 249
Fresh Layered Salad, 74
Fried Zucchini Ribbons with Tzatziki, 236
Friedenberg, Kathie, 36
Fries, Green Bean, 146
frying oil temperature, 147

garnishing drinks, 168
gazpacho from leftover salad, 271
Gin & Tonic, Earl Grey, 186
Gin Cocktail, Pomegranate-Rosemary, 217
Ginger Cream, 172
Gingerbread Cookies, Fox, 272
Ginger-Cucumber Margarita, 230
Ginger-Lime Syrup, 233
Ginger-Tangerine Sparkler, 248
Ginger-Tangerine Syrup, 248
glossary of hunting terms & phrases, 276–79
Gluten-Free Walnut Rosemary Coconut Cake, 225
Gnocchi with Veal Marsala, 219
Goat Cheese & Herb–Stuffed Piquanté Peppers, 250
Golden Mushroom Soup, 119
Golden Potato Gratin, 41
golden syrup, 81
granola bars, 81
Gratin, Carrots, 160
Gratin, Golden Potato, 41
Green Bean Fries, 146
Green Goddess Dressing, 37
Greener Partners, 7
Grilled Loin Lamb Chops with Mint Pesto, 38
Grilled Peaches with Serrano Ham, 218
Grilled Pork Tenderloin with Apricot & Horseradish Sauce, 188

Hare, Horace, 16, *18*
Hash Browns & Roasted Peppers, 178
Hazelnut Dark Chocolate Tart, 111
Hearty Skillet Chicken, 205
history of Radnor Hunt, 14–19, *44, 84–85*, 129
Hollandaise Sauce, 177, 222

homemade breadcrumbs, 125
Homemade Coffee Liqueur, 126
Homemade Dill Pickles, 171
Homemade Grenadine, 62
horses, about, 25, 37, 61, 97, 109, 116, 153, 159, 199, 229, 230, 238, 261
hounds, about, 25, 83, 115, 153, 159, 167, 199, 229, 247, 261
The Hounds Foundation, 7
hunting terms & phrases, 276–79

Infused Earl Grey Gin, 186
Irish Oatmeal Brûlée with Ginger Cream, 172

Jackson, Roy, 16, *84–85*
jerk seasoning, 144
Julep, Devon, 200

Key Lime Pie, 259
Kirkwood Preserve, *227*

Lamb Lettuce Cups, Moroccan, 202
The Laurels Preserve, *254–55*
Layered Salad, Fresh, 74
Lemon & Garlic with Broccolini, 88
Lemonade, 48
Lettuce Cups, Moroccan Lamb, 202
Leverton, Will, *17*
Lime-Ginger Syrup, 233
liqueurs. *See* beverages
Loin Lamb Chops, Grilled, with Mint Pesto, 38

Macadamia & Arugula Salad, with Green Goddess Dressing, 34
Mâche Salad with French Vinaigrette, 249
mains
    Belgian Beef Stew, 158
    Calypso Turkey Sliders, 144
    Chicken Cashew Chili, 73
    Coq au Vin, 105
    Côte de Boeuf, 91

Grilled Loin Lamb Chops with Mint Pesto, 38
Grilled Pork Tenderloin with Apricot & Horseradish Sauce, 188
Hearty Skillet Chicken, 205
Irish Oatmeal Brûlée with Ginger Cream, 172
Poached Eggs on Brioche with Spinach, Spicy Bacon & Béarnaise Sauce, 175
Red Wine–Braised Short Ribs, 122
Sausage Shepherd's Pie, 141
Southern Tomato Pie, 256
Tortellini Chicken Alfredo, 267
Veal Marsala with Gnocchi, 219
Venison Chili, 143
make-ahead recipes, 61. *See also individual recipes*
Malone, Booth, 235
Malted Milk Ball Cake, 163
Maple Rosemary Bourbon Sour, 98
Margarita, Cucumber-Ginger, 230
Mather, Charles E., *19*
Mather, John, *18*
Meigs, Arthur, 16–17
Mint Pesto, 38
Molded Egg Salad, Appetizer, Retro, 65
Moran, Elizabeth "Betty," 5
Moroccan Lamb Lettuce Cups, 202
Moscow Mule, 263
Mrs. Moran's Brushwood Stables, *4–5*
Mushroom Soup, Golden, 119
Mushroom Tart, Creamy, 157
Mustard Vinaigrette, 162

Natural Lands, 7, *274–75*
Nuts, Sweet & Spicy, Mixed, 29

Oatmeal Brûlée, with Ginger Cream, Irish, 172
Oatmeal Chocolate Chip Pecan Cookies, 56

Paprika Dressing, 52
Party Potatoes, 108
pasta
    Easy Summer Pasta, 241
    Pasta with Pancetta & Peas, 253
    Tortellini Chicken Alfredo, 267
    Truffle Pasta, 55
Pâté, Chutney Cheese, 187
Pea Risotto, Spring, 190
Peaches, Grilled, with Serrano Ham, 218
Pecan Chocolate Bourbon Bread Pudding, 149

Pecan Oatmeal Chocolate Chip Cookies, 56
Pecans, Blue Cheese, 133
Peppadew peppers, 250
The Perfect Rob Roy, 84
Pesto, Mint, 38
Pew, Benjamin 16
Pickles, Homemade Dill, 171
Piquanté Peppers, Goat Cheese & Herb-Stuffed, 250
pizzas & savory tarts
    Creamy Mushroom Tart, 157
    Pizza Dough, 138
    Truffle Pizza, 138
Plantation Field, *112–13*
Planter's Punch, 62
Poached Eggs on Brioche with Spinach, Spicy Bacon & Béarnaise Sauce, 175
Polo Punch, 48
Pomegranate-Rosemary Gin Cocktail, 217
Poppy Seed Almond Cake with Balsamic Berries, 210
Pork Tenderloin, Grilled, with Apricot & Horseradish Sauce, 188
Potato Gratin, 41
pounding meat, 221
prime rib, 91
Prosciutto, Arugula & Provolone Rolls, 238

Radnor Hunt Pub, *131*
Radnor Hunt racecourse, *58–59*
ras el hanout, 203
Red Wine–Braised Short Ribs, 122
Red Wine Sorbet, 92
Reeve, J. Stanley, *44*
Retro Molded Egg Salad Appetizer, 65
Rice Salad, Sicilian, 179
rimming glasses, 168
Risotto, Corn & Saffron, 124
Risotto, Spring Pea, 190
Roasted Brussels Sprouts with Bacon & Sriracha Aïoli, 191
Roasted Cauliflower with Hollandaise Sauce, 222

Roasted Corn Salad, 70
Roasted Peppers & Hash Browns, 178
roasted red peppers, 69
Roasted Sweet Potatoes & Bacon, 206
roasting chestnuts, 88
Rob Roy, The Perfect, 84
Romaine, Clementines & Cabbage Salad, 104
Rosemary, Tomato & Cannellini Soup, 33
rosemary extract, 226
Rosemary Maple Bourbon Sour, 98
Rosemary Syrup, 225
Rosemary Walnut Coconut Cake, Gluten-Free, 225
Rosemary-Blackberry Rum Cocktail, 26
Rosemary-Blackberry Syrup, 26
Rosemary–Brown Sugar Syrup, 217
Rosemary-Pomegranate Gin Cocktail, 217
Rum Cocktail, Blackberry-Rosemary, 26
Rumtini, Apple Cider 130
Russian Tea Cakes, 196

Saffron & Corn Risotto, 124
salads & dressings
    Arugula & Macadamia Salad with Green Goddess Dressing, 34
    Boone Salad, 271
    Brussels Sprout Salad with Mustard Vinaigrette, 162
    Clementines, Cabbage & Romaine Salad, 104
    French Vinaigrette, 249
    Fresh Layered Salad, 74
    Green Goddess Dressing, 37
    Mâche Salad with French Vinaigrette, 249
    Mustard Vinaigrette, 162
    Paprika Dressing, 52
    Roasted Corn Salad, 70
    Sicilian Rice Salad, 179
    Spinach Salad with Paprika Dressing, 52
    Tarragon Vinaigrette, 209
    Watermelon, Arugula & Feta Salad, 242
sauces, savory & sweet
    Apricot & Horseradish Sauce, 188
    Béarnaise Sauce, 176
    Caramel Sauce for Bread Pudding, 149, 150
    Caramel Sauce for Brownies, 77
    Ginger Cream, 172
    Hollandaise Sauce, 177, 222

Mint Pesto, 38
    Sriracha Aïoli, 191
    Tzatziki, 236
    Yogurt-Sriracha Sauce, 202
Sausage Shepherd's Pie, 141
Scotch Eggs, 137
Seared Sesame Tuna Bites, 102
Serrano Ham with Grilled Peaches, 218
Sesame Tuna Bites, 102
Short Ribs, Red Wine–Braised, 122
Shrimp Creole, 180
Sicilian Rice Salad, 179
sides. See also salads & dressings
    Asparagus with Hazelnuts & Tarragon Vinaigrette, 209
    Broccolini with Lemon & Garlic, 88
    Carrots au Gratin, 160
    Corn & Saffron Risotto, 124
    Creole Shrimp, 180
    Farmers' Market Succotash, 268
    Fried Zucchini Ribbons with Tzatziki, 236
    Golden Potato Gratin, 41
    Green Bean Fries, 146
    Hash Browns & Roasted Peppers, 178
    Homemade Dill Pickles, 171
    Party Potatoes, 108
    Roasted Brussels Sprouts with Bacon & Sriracha Aïoli, 191
    Roasted Cauliflower with Hollandaise Sauce, 222
    Roasted Sweet Potatoes & Bacon, 206
    Spring Pea Risotto, 190
    Zucchini Cakes, 125
Simple Syrup, 154
Skillet Chicken, Hearty, 205
Sour Cream Coffee Cake, 183
Southern Tomato Pie, 256
Sparkler, Tangerine-Ginger, 248
Spicy Bloody Mary, 168
Spinach Salad with Paprika Dressing, 52
spreads. See dips & spreads
Spring Pea Risotto, 190
squeezing lemons, 48
Sriracha Aïoli, 191
Sriracha-Yogurt Sauce, 202
standing rib roast, 91
stirrup cup, 25
substituting flour, 213, 226
Succotash, Farmers' Market, 268
Summer Pasta, Easy, 241
Sun-Dried Tomato & Caper Tapenade, 116

Sweet & Spicy Mixed Nuts, 29
Sweet Potato & Chestnut Soup, 87
Sweet Potatoes, Roasted, & Bacon, 206
syrups
    Blackberry-Rosemary Syrup, 26
    Ginger-Lime Syrup, 233
    Homemade Grenadine, 62
    Rosemary Syrup, 225
    Rosemary–Brown Sugar Syrup, 217
    Simple Syrup, 154
    Tangerine-Ginger Syrup, 248

"Tallyho" origin, 215
Tangerine-Ginger Sparkler, 248
Tangerine-Ginger Syrup, 248
Tapenade, Sun-Dried Tomato & Caper, 116
Tarragon Vinaigrette, 209
Tea Cakes, Russian, 196
Texas Caviar Dip, 68
toasting coconut, 245; nuts, 34, 209
Tomato, Cannellini & Rosemary Soup, 33
Tomato Pie, Southern, 256
Tortellini Chicken Alfredo, 267
Truffle Pasta, 55
Truffle Pizza, 138
Tuna Bites, Seared Sesame, 102
Turkey Sliders, Calypso, 144
Tzatziki, 236

vanilla, 101
Veal Marsala with Gnocchi, 219
Venison Chili, 143

Watermelon, Arugula & Feta Salad, 242
Whiskey Sour, Classic, 154
White Russian Cocktail, 126
Willistown Conservation Trust, 7, 113, 227
Wine Sorbet, Red, 92

Yogurt-Sriracha Sauce, 202

Zucchini Cakes, 125
Zucchini Ribbons, Fried, 236

It is customary, regardless of the time of day, to wish a "good night" to all at the end of a day of hunting. Therefore, we wish you all a good night!